THE MARRIAGE TEST

THE
MARRIAGE TEST

Our 40 Dates Before "I Do"

Jill Andres

AND

Brook Silva-Braga

BERKLEY BOOKS, NEW YORK

BERKLEY

An imprint of Penguin Random House LLC
375 Hudson Street, New York, New York 10014

Library of Congress Cataloging-in-Publication Data

Andres, Jill.
The marriage test : our 40 dates before "I do" / Jill Andres and Brook Silva-Braga.
        p.   cm.
ISBN 978-0-425-28275-5 (paperback)
    1. Andres, Jill.   2. Silva-Braga, Brook.   3. Man-woman relationships.
4. Dating (Social customs)   5. Courtship.   6. Marriage.   I. Silva-Braga, Brook.
II. Title.
HQ801.A584 2016
306.7—dc23
2015030695

PUBLISHING HISTORY
Berkley trade paperback edition / February 2016

PRINTED IN THE UNITED STATES OF AMERICA

10 9 8 7 6 5 4 3 2 1

Cover art by Sarah Wilkins.
Cover design by Danielle Abbiate.
Back cover author photos by B. Silva-Braga.
Interior text design by Kristin del Rosario.

Penguin is committed to publishing works of quality and integrity.
In that spirit, we are proud to offer this book to our readers;
however, the story, the experiences, and the words
are the authors' alone.

Penguin
Random
House

AUTHORS' NOTE

Everything in the book really happened, though we sometimes altered chronology and on a few occasions punched up dialogue for the sake of keeping you interested. We also changed some people's names and/or identifying information in exchange for their honesty and/or continued friendship.

CONTENTS

INTRODUCTION

BROOK: I remember sitting on the couch, staring at a dead TV, trying to breathe. "You hungry?" Jill asked when she walked into our apartment. She was just getting back from a friend's bachelorette weekend in New Orleans. "We should talk first," I said. She put down her bag and I could see the color drain from her face until it matched mine. "Let me go to the bathroom first," she said, and I sat there waiting, counting the breaths until I blew up our lives.

At that point we'd been together for nearly four years in the best, most serious relationship either of us had known. A mutual friend invited us to the same small party and Jill was the first person I noticed, the energetic, strong-willed center of the room. Blue eyes and brown curls. I was smitten. Within a couple of months we were inseparable, hanging out six nights a week all over New York City. She was funny and smart and we liked the same trashy bars and could talk all night about that science story in the *Times* or why Mexican food sucks on the East Coast.

At first it was platonic, then it wasn't; either way it was like magic just being together. You know that scene in a rom-com where the couple first meets? Every day felt like that. "Dad, how do you know when you're really in love?" "Son, you'll know when you know." I never had that conversation with my dad, but you get the idea. I knew. After three years together she was still the best friend I'd ever had. And we moved in together. And people thought we were getting married. And all along the whole thing had been fucked.

Sitting on the couch, I couldn't quite say why it was fucked. I could only just barely tell that it was. It's awfully hard to look at a relationship honestly when you're still in it. After the fact, we all pretend the problems were easy to see. But when you're still trying to keep it alive—because of love or comfort or fear—everything seems curable. For a long time we were stuck in that dark, undiagnosed place. Nothing is perfect. How good is it really supposed to be before we commit our lives to each other? How do we know which side of that line we're on?

Picking a partner is the most important decision any of us will ever make, but how are we supposed to make it? Being in love is obviously a good start, but the things that ultimately wreck marriages—money and monogamy, career and kids—are hard to practice for until you're actually hitched. *What if she spends too much? What if I'm a bad dad?* You can be together for years without ever truly auditioning each other for the Big Job.

And that's what Jill and I did. We comfortably drifted along, talking about that article we just read and why East Coast burritos are bad. We stoically ignored that our relationship was dying—until Jill came out of the bathroom with a box of tissues to sit with me on the couch for our funeral. Four good years, gone like that. They were garbage now, a mistake, a waste, something to be vaguely embarrassed about. And the scariest part was, we just as easily could have gotten married without realizing what a bad idea that was.

JILL: Brook and I sat there on the couch and cried for a long while. His decision to end it was like the last chapter of a mystery novel: At first it was surprising and then I realized the whole story had been a collection of hints pointing to this end. First let's fondly remember the misdirections: We loved each other more than we'd ever loved anyone else and had an incredible amount of fun. We shared adventures across five New York boroughs and four continents. Best of all, we were super-positive influences on each other. Brook nudged me toward grad school, I helped him plant roots. We were, I swear, *great* together in so many ways.

But a couple can fall in love and stay in love and still be wrong for each other. Even during the best of times, there were quiet reservations, things we felt but would never say. Like the fact that we struggled to connect sexually. We were always affectionate, but for some reason that failed to translate into a fulfilling sex life. *That's just what happens when you go from being platonic friends to partners*, I told myself. Or the fact I never really felt optimistic about our future. Friends would say they'd never heard anyone in such a strong long-term relationship use the phrase "*If* things work out between us" so often. *Being conservative is a normal reaction to falling in love, right?*

Pairing off may be humanity's core function, but we're still totally shit at it. This is where I should mention the 50 percent divorce rate. Except the U.S. divorce rate is probably closer to 40 percent. The precise number is impossible to say because the data is poorly kept and no one knows what percentage of people married two years ago will end up divorcing. But a University of Michigan economist projected that if current trends continued, only about 35 percent of marriages would end in divorce.

The divorce rate has actually been inching lower since 1980, which sounds like good news until you hear how we've done it. For decades Americans got married at roughly the same average age: twenty-four for men, twenty-one for woman. But since 1980 the age has gone way up; it's now over twenty-nine for men and twenty-seven for women. Our generation seems to think we can avoid repeating the baby boomers' mistakes by putting off commitment.

At thirty-four and thirty-one, Brook and I were precocious examples. I had always figured marriage could wait. Why stop traveling, going out, and building a career? *I'm having fun dating this guy, let's not rush it*. Marriage could wait a little longer. And a little longer.

It seems to me both trends—divorcing and dithering—are driven by marriage's cruel paradox: It's really hard to know if you've chosen the right person until you've already married them.

The night Brook and I broke up, we were able to talk in a way we'd always avoided when we were a couple. We told each other stuff that had been too hard or awkward before. Even the sex stuff. We had come so close to ending up together without ever mustering the courage to face our true shortcomings as a couple.

I left town to go backpacking through Asia; Brook took over the lease on our apartment. We moved on, we dated other people, we rarely spoke.

And that probably would have been the last sentence of our story if I hadn't received a note from Brook about a year later: "Hey, I'm getting kicked out of the old apartment," he wrote. "Gonna have a New Year's Eve party as a send-off. You should come!" It seemed like a bad idea. *But all my friends will be there*, I told myself.

At midnight those friends were confused why I wasn't huddled around the TV counting down to the New Year. I was on the roof, watching fireworks over the Hudson River, kissing Brook. He'd taken me aside earlier in the night and said he missed me.

I knew it violated the breakup handbook, but over the next few months we started casually seeing each other again. Eight months later, when Brook moved south for a job with the *Washington Post*, we took an even bigger step: I followed him to D.C. and we moved back in together. Brook and Jill, version 2.0.

And it felt different—healthier, more open. Old patterns changed. I felt like Brook appreciated me in a new way. And I believed he'd become more worthy of my appreciation. The good stuff hadn't really changed; we still had as much fun as ever. And I really did think (and most days hoped) Brook could be my husband. But let's be honest: I'd already thought that once before.

BROOK: I guess we came up with this project because we were afraid to make the same mistake twice. The idea came to us on a sunny summer evening after work, in a rented kayak on the Potomac River. It was one of those warm and easy days—good weather, good jobs, good health—the kind of perfect moment we're all dumb enough to think might last forever if we just keep waiting for the right person. Or, if we're sick of waiting, it's the kind of blue-sky day that tricks an incompatible couple into saying "I do."

In the distance the sun was setting on our adopted city, the sky around the Washington Monument turning a burnt orange. We had been together a year in this new relationship and it seemed to be headed somewhere serious. But before we took that big step toward forever, maybe we should make sure this time really was different. Maybe we should make sure we weren't avoiding or ignoring something important.

"What if we made like an obstacle course of challenges to see if we'd be good at being married?" Jill suggested.

"That would be hilarious. We could borrow a baby for the weekend and see if it survived."

"What if we went on a date with our exes?"

"Oh my God, that would be so awkward," I said.

"Do you think they'd do it? Don't all your exes hate you?"

"At least one of them doesn't," I joked. Jill dipped her oar against the current and splashed me across the face.

It sounded like the kind of fun, quirky adventure we'd always been good at. And honestly, at the time, we were naïve enough to think we'd pass with flying colors. We got out of the kayak, grabbed our phones, and typed out as many of the ideas as we could remember.

Swap credit cards for a month.

Spend a week grading each other's performance in the bedroom.

Trade phones for a weekend.

Over the next few weeks we asked friends and family to contribute date ideas. We defined "date" liberally; any activity they thought would help us reach a decision was fair game, and their suggestions seemed to cover every possible pitfall. The ideas also seemed to reveal a lot about their own relationships: a recently engaged woman kept suggesting more adventurous sex, my chronically single coworker was fixated on in-laws, and a married friend who was about to become a dad seemed to suggest we should see other people. We scaled down his idea and turned it into our first activity: speed dating.

We realized pretty quickly that they were more than funny stunts. The dates would help force the "should we or shouldn't we" decision we had continued to put off. They would help us understand if our relationship was built to last by actively simulating the strains of marriage.

Most of the ideas fell into a handful of thematic buckets, so we started to group them and soon found ourselves with ten categories, a kind of Daters' Decathlon. And then we gave our Marriage Test the ultimate stakes. If it went well, we'd spend our lives together. If not, we were done for good.

Trust

DATE #1

Speed Dating

JILL: He wasn't actually flirting with her, was he? Brook sat ten feet in front of me smiling at a cute, skinny brunette with hipster glasses and a bob. We had mapped out forty activities to test our relationship, starting with the most basic question: Would we rather be with someone else? So, speed dating. It had sounded like a good idea before we left our apartment one Friday night and walked separately through the rain to a Hyatt hotel. The organizers hastily dashed expectations of romance or glamour by herding us into a sterile basement room that betrayed a whiff of breakfast buffet. But here we were, dating other people, maybe for the last time.

Tables for two were scattered across the room. But like every other place where adults are seriously attempting to pair off, there were more women here than men. So the ladies took turns sitting alone and now I was the lucky girl sipping a bourbon, waiting five minutes for my next date. I had a front-row seat as Brook joined the hipster girl at the next table. Bad timing.

The speed dates so far had been legitimate, harmless fun; they'd gone by in a flash. But five minutes lasts longer when you're sitting alone watching your boyfriend flirt; in five minutes, I realized, you can sing most of "American Pie." In five minutes you can drain a glass of bourbon.

Maybe it was the liquid courage, but I suddenly felt an urge to clear my throat and remind the room that no one was going to find their soul mate in the breakfast buffet room. First off, there was obviously no such thing as a soul mate. If only one of the planet's 3.5 billion men were meant for me, I would have rescued a cat and adopted an ice cream diet years ago. I mean, how did people who believed in soul mates even get up in the morning? But knowing there was no "perfect guy" waiting for me to find him didn't make picking a partner any easier. It probably made it harder. What was the right standard for deciding the guy you were with was good enough? That was a much harder problem than simply waiting to meet the flawless, no-compromise man of your imagination.

The flawed, some-compromise man I already shared an apartment with was still flirting with the hipster. Brook looked younger than thirty-four, with a full head of wavy brown hair. It was September and long runs around the National Mall had bronzed his Mediterranean skin. She lifted her hand to finger her necklace. *How were these five minutes not over?* It felt like hotel guests could line up for their steamed eggs at any moment!

I didn't want to stare at Brook, so I tried to distract myself with the notes from my dates so far. *First guy: good-looking, athletic 20-something*, I had written. "Yeah, I played football in college," he conceded. I swooned. Then there was a smart-seeming thirty-year-old who had just moved to Washington from Kabul. We talked about how both cities had changed (I'd done an earlier stint in D.C. after college), though comparing the District of Columbia and Afghanistan made it hard to complain about Washington. But after those early high points it quickly went downhill: a guy who gave one-word answers as he gazed into the distance over my shoulder, a gentleman who seemingly trimmed two decades off his age to qualify for the event, and another who should have picked his clothes from a different part of his closet.

But maybe I was being harsh. What did they think when they sat across from me? Did they notice the yellow specks around my blue irises from too many summers at the neighborhood pool, the frazzled loops of chestnut hair my mom had never known how to brush, the one fake tooth half a shade lighter than the rest? I lost the tooth on a rafting trip in Uganda at the violent start of the Nile. Brook was on the raft with me. "Yeah, you lost a tooth," he said calmly. "You're going to be okay."

I folded up my sheet of notes and tried to picture each of the six guys I'd met so far sitting next to me in the raft in Uganda. Then I imagined them barhopping with me in New York, holding my infant child, making love to me. I looked up at Brook and realized I'd rather be picturing him. If not for him, it was hard to even imagine myself in the raft in Uganda. That was sort of a bad example because I'd like to have that tooth back, but still. Every time my tongue touched the seam of my fake incisor, I was reminded how different my life would be if I'd never dated Brook.

I was twenty-four when I took a weekend trip to Boston and met him at that party. We were both about to move to New York; Brook was returning there after a year traveling around the world making a documentary. A trip like that was something I'd always dreamed of

but with Brook, daydreams had a way of becoming real-life itinerar-
ies. It didn't have to be as grand as an international trip. It could be
anything unexpected, off-kilter, out of your comfort zone. One Saturday we gathered friends for a "Five Borough Bar Crawl" and rode
the subway all across the city, finding little corners of Staten Island
and Queens we'd otherwise never visit. Instead of a grocery store, we
shopped at a group of stalls under the Manhattan Bridge selling
obscure Asian vegetables at impossibly low prices. On the first warm
weekend of the year, we'd take the subway to the northern tip of
Manhattan and walk the thirteen miles down to Wall Street.

We kind of stumbled into dating each other. At first he said he
wasn't interested in having a girlfriend and I was okay with that; I
was still trying to settle into New York. But after a few months
exploring the city together, he cooked me dinner one night and told
me he wanted to start dating. I figured, *Why not?* I mean, we liked the
same stuff, he was handsome and smart. How could a girl turn that
down? Plus, dating seemed not much different from our super-close
friendship, just more kissing and fewer lonely subway rides home.

Time just kind of slipped by, a weekend becoming a year; sneaking
into the movies to catch a double feature we didn't pay for, slipping
into China to work on a film we weren't quite licensed to shoot.

It was kind of great. It was like the second month of a relationship that's going really well, all that fun and excitement without
much worrying about where it's going. Because from the beginning
I assumed it wouldn't go anywhere.

Brook was in his twenties and didn't seem to be in any rush to
settle down with one special lady. And that was fine, at first. I didn't
mind if he couldn't totally commit because totally committing scared
me too. I adopted the posture of the cool, no-pressure girlfriend.

Even after we became exclusive I stayed chill. Yeah, maybe over time that emotional wall got tougher to maintain. But I maintained it! I didn't let myself worry about the pretty girl flirting with him at the bar. *Whatever, he'll come home with me tonight anyway.* Jealousy was so pathetic; normal girlfriends got jealous, but not me. I didn't see the point in pushing for changes in our relationship. Normal girlfriends were demanding, not me.

On a camping trip in New Hampshire about a year after we started dating, Brook and I found ourselves swimming in a little river on a perfect summer afternoon. We climbed up onto a sun-baked rock to dry off. It was romantic; I felt warm inside and out and wanted Brook to know.

"Hey, can I tell you something?" I said, grabbing his hand.

"Sure, what's up?"

"I . . . I . . ." I tried to channel my inner courage but chickened out. "I think we should build a campfire tonight." I wanted to finally say *I love you*, to explain that I thought of him as more than my adventure buddy. But I couldn't work up the nerve. It was six months later, a moment after he said it himself, that I finally got the words out. But even then we remained the couple who acted like they'd been dating two months as we celebrated our second anniversary.

Only later did I understand the message my silence and general ambivalence were sending Brook all those years: *I'm not invested in this so you don't have to be either.* It was a testament to how much we liked being around each other that we lasted as long as we did; the union of a commitment-averse guy and a no-demands girl.

Back in 2011, as I clutched that box of tissues on our couch, Brook said he had to break up with me because he had cheated. "Never get back together with me," he said. "If you do, I'll cheat on you again."

Now he was smiling at some random girl at table sixteen, and I wondered why we were putting ourselves through this.

BROOK: I'm going to be honest. Because why go through the trouble of doing these dates and writing about them if we're not honest? I know that means I'll sound like a bad guy some of the time because I've been a bad guy some of the time. But I did not perform inventive feats of asshole-dom, I mainly committed the sin of being *that guy*. I didn't want to be *that guy*, I didn't enjoy being *that guy*—actually, I spent a lot of energy trying not to be him, which only made it more depressing that I couldn't seem to pull it off. So I'm going to write about what that was like and maybe it'll give you a better understanding of *that guy* in your life, maybe even if he's you.

So we sat in the Hyatt basement checking to see if we'd rather be single, and here's the truth: Sarah, the hipster girl sitting across from me at table sixteen, was easy to look at, smart, kind of funny. But she wasn't any kind of threat. I felt nothing. And feeling nothing felt *amazing*. To feel nothing while sitting across from an attractive woman was one of the great accomplishments of my life, and yes, I realize how pathetic that sounds. Did it make me immune to the charms of every woman on the planet, or even in this room? Probably not. Did it mean Jill and I were right for each other? Not necessarily. But I no longer felt like a fraud asking her to trust me.

That meant I had another chance with the best woman I'd ever met. But let's be honest about something else: You can't describe your girlfriend objectively. So I'll quote a guy who's known Jill since college: "She's the real-life version of a romantic comedy leading lady, the archetype that doesn't usually exist," he said. "Jill is the cool, fun, funny girl who's into sports and going on adventures.

She's the person you kind of imagine existing but then never actually meet."

That was the woman I couldn't make it work with the first time, for lots of reasons. But a big part of it was that I had this nagging need to scan every room, like the slow drip of a faucet that with every drop reminded me to see-what-else-was-out-there. It wasn't that I wanted to be with someone else; I wanted badly *not* to be with someone else, to be faithful to Jill, but I was standing in an empty swimming pool that started to fill up from all the drips. I couldn't admit that to Jill and she seemed to ignore it, even as the water slowly built up around me. When it finally lipped over my head and drowned our relationship, I was angry and sad but also relieved to not be trying to stay above the water anymore. I got drunk one night when Jill wasn't around and stumbled into the arms of a girl I remember almost nothing about. It was profoundly disappointing, but not surprising. That's why I told Jill not to get back together with me; I didn't know how to stop the pool from filling with water again.

I know no one wants to hear a bad boyfriend's excuses. So I say this next part carefully even though it's true: Jill and I worked as a team to create an unhealthy, dysfunctional relationship. We both failed to discuss our problems, to act like we had been dating for two months when really we were facing some pretty serious issues. I was responsible for killing our bad relationship, but we were both responsible for creating it. I wasn't sure Jill really understood that.

But we were doing these dates because we believed our relationship was different this time. And I believed I was different. The point of the test was to find out if we really were.

I rotated to the next table and Lily was sitting there, a bit rumpled and seemingly distracted. I was never going to be attracted to Lily, but I still wanted to make a good impression. As a journalist, I liked to think I could build rapport with strangers pretty quickly, but Lily's speed-dating technique could best be described as *uncooperative witness*—not quite openly hostile but clearly annoyed with the proceedings. "What do you do?" I queried.

"I watch horror movies. But there aren't any good ones anymore."

"I don't know much about horror movies. What are the old ones I should check out?"

"Oh, I don't know," she offered. Our five minutes were up.

Then, at table eighteen, I sat across from Kayla. *Oh no.* She smiled with these big turquoise eyes as ribbons of blond hair framed her dewy skin. A hint of natural rose flushed her cheeks; a floral silk top draped off the ridge of her collarbone. Kayla had been plucked from a toothpaste commercial. For the first time in months, I heard that awful, familiar drip. It was impossible to sit there and not want her to like me. If the toothpaste girl leaned across the table and tried to kiss me, I would feel differently about myself. Better about myself. *Why was that?*

When the most famous cheater of the last half century was asked why he betrayed his vows, he gave a pretty bullshit answer. "I did [it] for the worst possible reason," Bill Clinton said. "Because I could." What kind of explanation is that? There are *lots* of things you could do, Bill. There has to be a better reason why you did that one!

But over the years I gave a lot of thought to Clinton's answer, because I struggled to come up with a better explanation myself.

I went to college at New York University, surrounded by a million Greenwich Village bars that didn't care how old you were. At Bar None the little plastic cups of beer were a dollar until midnight; at any hour our fondest wish was to meet someone to get naked with. When you're nineteen, you don't spend a lot of time analyzing why you want to go home with a girl, but when it actually started happening I noticed something kind of troubling. As soon as it reached a certain point—pretty much once the girl agreed to go home with me—I lost most of my interest. I still enjoyed the rest of it, but I somehow knew the point had been the first part. I mainly wanted to see if I could get her to say yes.

Over time, through no fault of my own, I achieved some small measure of emotional maturity. I dated women for good and adult reasons—we liked the same writers or played the same sport or got the same jokes. But liking them, and occasionally even loving them, didn't end that other impulse, that moment of seeing someone across a room and wondering *if I could*. I think what Clinton and I wanted (more than love or friendship or even physical enjoyment) was to have that little hole in our ego tickled by the fact that she said yes. For a lot of guys that hole couldn't be filled any other way. Clinton's bullshit answer made more sense the older I got.

"I just moved here from Pittsburgh." The toothpaste girl smiled. "I'm working at NIH." That was Washington-speak for the National Institutes for Health; she was a sexy scientist. *Did someone plant this woman here?* In my brain, I easily made a long list of things I loved about Jill, of the many ways she must be better than the toothpaste girl. *Imagine how boring Ms. Toothpaste would be after a month*, I told myself. *Or five years.* When I thought about it that way, I almost wasn't tempted.

When the round of dates was finished we were encouraged to mingle in the hotel bar. I found Jill and bought her a drink; we were still pretending not to know each other. She started telling me about her dates and asking about mine. Then she grabbed my arm and held it; I guess she was done being single. She said to meet her for dinner when I finished my beer, and a moment later she was gone from the bar altogether. As I waited for the check, Kayla came over and we started talking. She mentioned leadingly that she was about to meet up with friends. I reminded myself how boring she'd be after a month.

When I was a kid, my family took a vacation to this little island off the coast of Georgia where loggerhead turtles nest. In the middle of the night we went down to the shore with flashlights. As the hatchlings scampered toward the water, ghost crabs raced across the beach and stabbed the turtles to death. I remember the park ranger saying how the crabs would take one bite of the hatchling and spit it out. Then they'd kill another, only to discover it tasted bad too. The ghost crabs never learned. They did this useless, destructive thing because they could. It took me a lot of years and a lot of drunk talks with conflicted guys to understand how many of us were ghost crabs—journalists and presidents whose deepest instincts could not be wished away.

I signed the credit card slip and told Kayla it was nice to meet her. It felt good to be better than a shithead crab; I had done more to change than just wish. It was a warm late-summer night and the rain had changed to a light mist that covered my face as I walked up Tenth Street. By the time I found Jill at an outdoor table at the restaurant below our apartment, I was dry.

DATE #2

Phone Swap

BROOK: I handed her my iPhone as soon as I sat down at the restaurant. We had talked about starting our next date—trading phones for a weekend—sometime "soon," and I figured "soon" could be now.

"Do you really think I'm going to let you just jump into the next date?" Jill laughed. "How do you know I even want to go forward?

There were some nice guys at speed dating." Her phone dinged on the table with an e-mail. Our fellow daters were able to message us and already were. "You gonna get that?" I asked. She spun the phone to see who had written but left the message unopened.

"The girl with the glasses at the next table was cute," she said. "I was jealous." Those were words I don't think I'd ever heard her say. Jill had always insisted she didn't experience jealousy.

"Yeah, there were a few cute girls there," I said. "And smart too. Some of them just moved here; I think that's why they were single."

"Makes sense. Gotta scoop them up at the airport. The guys were definitely better than I expected. Who knew these people were hiding at speed-dating events? We need to tell our single friends."

"So you were jealous," I said. "That's kind of sweet."

"Well, the point of the date was to see if we were tempted."

"Well, yeah, but after five minutes?"

"You never know," Jill said.

"If you're Mark Zuckerberg and someone offers you ownership of the next can't-miss Internet company in exchange for all your shares of Facebook, do you take the deal?" I took a sip of beer for dramatic effect. "Of course not, you already own Facebook!"

"Are you comparing me to Facebook? You don't even use Facebook."

My phone dinged. "Give me that," she laughed. Clearly we had passed Date #1 and were moving on.

Swapping phones was no joke, though several friends thought it was. They didn't think it was a *ha-ha* joke, but a *you can't be serious* joke. "What's the next date, having a threesome while combining your retirement accounts?"

One friend estimated his own relationship would survive the phone swap "for roughly ten minutes." Yes, trading phones with Jill might be dangerous, but I actually looked forward to it. It was a chance to show her I had nothing to hide.

After dinner, back in our apartment, Jill and I had access to basically all our communications from the last many months. How do private investigators stay in business? What can they tell you that your partner's phone can't? The two barriers to riffling through someone's phone are (1) their PIN and (2) your scruples.

As for the first, Jill and I already knew each other's PINs because she had used my phone to look up something on Wikipedia or I had borrowed hers to navigate to a restaurant. That's the world of almost-privacy a lot of couples live in, protected by a passcode their partner could probably guess. So that left scruples.

Jill had scruples, and I trusted she hadn't gone through my phone. I knew I hadn't gone through hers. But now we were snooping, so I started flipping through her apps and it was kind of a rush. I found a stash of unopened voicemails and feigned outrage, not over their content but because Jill still hadn't listened to them—I obsess over clean, empty inboxes.

"Just go ahead and delete them," she said. Jill worked as a business consultant, and the stream of incoming messages was more than she could keep up with. But before deleting, I gave a listen. Among the voicemails she had ignored: a very old birthday greeting, an update on a delayed flight, and a guy named Wolf asking when he could pick up his missing laptop. Wolf had called nine weeks ago!

Next up: her collection of unread e-mails, starting with a spam report from work. "Yeah, just delete that too," she said. Instead, I read through it and found a digital Starbucks gift certificate someone had sent her months before. Read your e-mails, Jill!

Maybe we should have established some boundaries about how far back we were allowed to look or which apps we could open. But we didn't; everything was fair game. So, yes, I searched Jill's messages and e-mails from the year we were broken up. (I am not proud of this fact). They were about what you'd expect from an eligible, single lady in New York. The juiciest ones thanked a guy "for a fun night (and morning)" or praised another for being "the first person who has successfully picked me up on the subway."

Jill and I had been very open about how we'd spent that year, so most of the guys in her inbox were characters she had mentioned as part of one story or another. But it was painful to stumble onto a couple of inconsistencies, like pillow talk with a mutual acquaintance she had told me she wasn't into. There was no rational reason to be upset about what she did while we were apart, but the e-mails were impossible to un-read. Weeks later I worked up the nerve to call her out on misleading me about the guy we both knew. "Oh yeah," she said, "that did happen."

I couldn't be mad at her for keeping it from me, or for doing it, but jealousy isn't a rational feeling. And that was probably a good thing to remember as I worked to keep Jill's trust in our new relationship.

JILL: I unlocked Brook's latest iPhone and chuckled. For a guy whose job involved using complicated video equipment, he was not very careful with his things. He had cracked his first iPhone the day he got it and seemed to need a new device every few months. His old texts and voicemails were mostly stored on a memory chip in a landfill somewhere. I didn't mind, though; unlike Brook I didn't really want to read stuff from when we were broken up. But I knew I had to look through some of what was on his phone, for his sake and for mine.

Since Brook's travel documentaries aired on TV and he hosted a video show for the *Washington Post*, he received lots of unsolicited messages and I guess I worried there might be people (cough, women, cough) he was in constant touch with but never mentioned. If I was honest with myself, worrying about women pursuing Brook felt familiar. I'd just never done anything about it before.

So sitting on our couch with his phone in my hands was a profound shift. This was my first time snooping, but if my unscientific polling is accurate, virtually every man reading this book should assume that his phone, computer, and browsing history have been compromised. What surprised me when I talked to girlfriends about this wasn't the fact that they snooped, but rather that they were totally unapologetic about it!

"It's really a form of relationship hygiene," one married friend told me. "It gives me a chance to know what's bothering him and help him deal with it." A likely excuse, but the truth was she wanted to know if he was messing around. To make sure their men weren't violating their trust, many women went ahead and violated their men's trust.

Plenty of them had their worst fears confirmed. One friend discovered a secret e-mail account her husband was using to communicate with his mistress. Another learned her fiancé had cheated during a friend's bachelor party years before. All terrible stuff they deserved to know and never would have learned without snooping. Several friends found it strange that this phone swap date was my first time looking through Brook's accounts, especially the friends who knew our history.

I had done my best to limit how many people knew that history. Being cheated on filled me with anger and sadness but, more than anything, with a lot of shame. I didn't want to look like the fool who had ended up with that kind of guy. I didn't want people to think I couldn't keep Brook's interest, like maybe it was my fault for not being pretty or interesting enough. Even just writing about it here brings back some of that shame.

After our breakup, I was certain I would never trust Brook again—even he told me not to! I knew I needed some time and distance before trusting anyone else either, so I began following the *Get Over the Bastard* guidebook society has so carefully created for women. I moved out of our shared apartment and, with three months until my new job started, decided to find somewhere cheaper than New York to clear my mind. I found a hut on the beach in Malaysia and spent some wonderfully lazy weeks eating mangoes and skinny-dipping with strangers. *Eat, Pray, Get Your Groove Back*. I returned to New York and was ready to start fresh.

And I did! I dated some good guys and some fun guys in New York. I had genuinely started to move on when Brook unexpectedly invited me to his New Year's Eve party and we rekindled things. For a while, even though being back together felt awesome, I kept my distance. We had already done fun and awesome once before and it led nowhere good.

But on one of the last nights before he moved out of the apartment, we sat on our old couch and Brook opened up in a way he never had in all the years we were together. He cried in my arms. It did nothing to change what he'd done. It didn't wipe away our unhealthy habits as a couple. But after knowing him as long as I had, I could tell *something* was different about him. And he promised that it was something that would make him a better partner. Maybe I was a fool; maybe I was falling for the same shit on a different day. Maybe I still had too many of my own issues to work through. But I decided we deserved to find out.

So here we were, his phone in my hands. *I've changed*, it said. Or maybe it said, *We've changed*. Because the point wasn't just that Brook had nothing to hide, but that now I was willing to look, I was willing to make demands.

I scrolled through his e-mails, stopping to skim whatever looked interesting. I clicked on a few names I didn't recognize, looked through his sent folder. I didn't see anything suspicious, but quite frankly his inbox was so cluttered with fantasy sports updates and discount camera offers that it was hard to thoroughly snoop.

On Saturday my investigation turned to the most likely of suspects; I unearthed a raft of Twitter and Facebook messages from "Friends" he'd never mentioned. But the responses were consistently short and innocent: "Hi [name], so glad you liked the film! Best of luck on your travels."

Forty-four hours into our forty-eight-hour swap, Brook was still buried in my phone reading who knows what. But I felt conflicted as I kept poking around his text messages. I'd seen enough to believe the phone was clean and I was losing my taste for the date. I barely wanted to read my own e-mails, let alone someone else's! And even more, I was starting to feel uncomfortable with how much Brook seemed to be searching through mine. There wasn't anything I was scared he would find, it just felt uncomfortable to lose so much of my privacy.

"Maybe we've seen enough," I said.

"Four more hours!" He barely looked up from my phone. "I'm only up to 2005," he joked.

I knew this was what I had signed up for, and if I backed out he might say I hadn't fully committed to the activity. I knew the *easiest* thing was to go along with the program, but I decided I had a demand to make.

"No. I think we're done now. This has been enough. Let's swap back." If his face flashed disappointment it was only for a second.

"Okay," he said.

Maybe I had backed out of the experiment a bit, but I felt we'd both made our point. Brook had given me his phone without reservation. And really, how many boyfriends would do that? Not many. And I appreciated that. It was basically what my girlfriends secretly demanded from their partners; they only trusted what they could verify, and so they snooped.

But "Phone Swap" convinced me of the opposite: I was recommitted to not snooping. It wasn't so I could go back to burying my head in the sand. Rather, this date reminded me that true trust was giving each other privacy and believing your partner would do right by you. Handing over our phones was a demonstration of trust, but so was handing them back.

DATE #3

Meet the Exes

JILL: On a trip back home to California, Brook and I drove through my old neighborhood and pulled into a familiar driveway. It was the house of my ex-boyfriend Will, my first love. Will and I dated through most of high school and part of college before breaking up for all the reasons nineteen-year-olds doing long-distance break up. Now, over a decade later, Brook and I were taking Will out to lunch. Who better than my first love to share my most-ingrained tendencies as a partner?

As we walked up to Will's front door, a flood of memories came rushing back. How many hundreds of times had I visited this house? It felt surreal—like two separate parts of my life colliding—as I rang the doorbell and waited for Will to answer with Brook standing next to me. Will and I had kept in sporadic touch over the years, but I wasn't sure he would be willing to meet up. (The first ex Brook con-tacted had backed out.) At first, it seemed like no one was going to answer the door. Then it finally swung open.

"You're early," Will said, and ran off to grab a belt.

"He was always late," I whispered to Brook. "That's probably one of the reasons I like that you're always on time." In the brief moment that they stood together in the doorway, I was surprised to see how similar Will and Brook looked—they were roughly the same height and build, with matching manes of wavy dark hair. I'd honestly never noticed before. Will finished getting dressed and reappeared in the entryway. We drove across town for Mexican food, took our super burritos to an empty table, and fired up a voice recorder.

"Ex-boyfriend checking in," Will said into the mic. "Very excit-ing so far."

"He's back in the picture, everybody," I added.

"People will want details of what went on here," Will continued. "Why was that afternoon so magical?"

"Probably the super burrito!" we said in unison.

That's just how Will and I had always been: high energy and in sync. You might think joking around with my ex-boyfriend in front of Brook would be awkward, but it really wasn't, at least not for me. More than anything, it was exhilarating to reconnect with someone who had played such an important role in my early life. There was even a time when I imagined a version of my life that ended with Will as my husband. What if I had gone to college closer to home? What if we had toughed out the long-distance thing a little longer? I had loved Will, at least in an eighteen-year-old kind of way, and he was a genuinely good guy. But I could tell right away that Will and I weren't long-lost soul mates. We might still get each other's sense of humor, but Brook was the one whose interests and life goals really matched mine.

Will had always been a loyal person and when Brook went to the bathroom he leaned forward. "So you said this is the second time you've dated; what happened the first time?" Before I could answer, Brook came back from the bathroom and we sat there in awkward silence for a moment.

Will finally jumped in. "Okay, this is my big question," he said. "Why exactly are you doing these dates? Do you need to do them because you're really not sure about your future?" It was the same question my dad had asked that morning. And I got it. Brook and I had known each other for years by this point; we'd already broken up and gotten back together. People thought we should have made a decision by now, and assumed it was a bad sign that we hadn't. From the outside it probably wasn't clear that even though we'd known each other for six years, the healthy, sustainable version of our relationship was barely one year old.

I looked at Brook and answered honestly, "I would say there's a ninety-seven percent chance I should marry you." I felt my cheeks instantly redden. It was the first time I'd ever said how close to sure I was.

"Ninety-seven percent sure?!" Brook exclaimed with a surprised look on his face.

"Wow, big numbers," Will chimed in.

Even I was surprised! I hadn't calculated my confidence in advance; it just kind of slipped out. But once I said the number, I realized it was true. Some of the confidence came from planning this project together and surviving those first two dates: not just seeing Brook's willingness to go through with them but his openness discussing how they made him feel. It was so different than the silent stomachaches of unspoken conflict during our first time together. Now it felt natural to admit I wanted things to work out with Brook, to have shed my old shrug-I-don't-care pose. And I hoped Brook saw my confidence as proof that I trusted him.

But there had probably been a day sometime in my senior year of high school when I was 97 percent sure about my future with Will. And that was the reason to do the dates. To see if that feeling survived the next thirty-seven tests.

BROOK: Will was basically the male Jill—quick with a joke, high energy. It was kind of weird to see someone so important to her past still have so much chemistry with her. I felt a bit like the outsider, not quite in on their secrets, not quite outgoing or energetic enough to keep up—it was hard enough to get a word in when there was *one* Jill to compete with. They struggled to remember why they had broken up, beyond growing apart after high school.

"I was exploring heroin," Will said. "Just kidding. Delete that from the book."

"Too late," Jill said. "It's already written. It's an auto-written book. We don't have time to write it."

It's strange to be the third wheel on a date with your live-in girlfriend. During a pause in their laugh parade, I asked Will about the good and bad parts of dating Jill back then.

"She was extremely sweet, funny. She was a good girlfriend, dedicated and dependable." Then his face turned very serious. "It's hard to find someone you can trust," he said.

He seemed to take half a beat to collect himself. "I never had one fight with Jill. That's one thing I always told my parents; I just never really fought with her." I was sure that was true. Jill and I hadn't fought the first time we dated either; that had been part of the problem.

"Well, what is something that you've discovered in someone else that you didn't find in Jill?" I asked.

"A lesser love for all things," he said with a laugh. "I dunno, you want me to find a drawback and I'm trying to think . . . Honestly we were like best friends. We just moved away and it was bad timing. I'm trying to think . . . something will come to me."

But it never did. After we drove back to Will's parents' house and dropped him off, it was just Jill and me in the car. Will's timing hadn't been good enough. A friend who married in his late twenties once described meeting your spouse as "the Slot Machine of Love," a game of chance where both partners had to decide never to pull the lever again. I knew how close I had come to missing my chance with Jill just like Will had.

When we got back home to D.C., we made plans to meet my ex-girl-friend in suburban Maryland. "Well, helloooo!" She was already waiting in the restaurant when we got there, seven months pregnant with her second kid. "Remember, you just can't use my real name," she said right away. "I do not need my name in your book, thanks. Call me Amanda or something."

"Amanda" was my last serious girlfriend before Jill, someone I actually thought I could spend my life with. Our first date was just after my twenty-fifth birthday and I can still remember us eating sandwiches in Bryant Park. She was so fun and easy to talk to. In that way she was a lot like Jill. I was smitten. Bowled over. Terrified.

Back then I didn't use words like *terrified*. I used words like *con-flicted*. All of a sudden I had a serious job and a serious girlfriend and I saw my life on train tracks to middle age, with offices and houses that got bigger and bigger, but a life that felt increasingly cramped. Like a lot of young men, I was afraid of commitment and unsure what to do. But I'd always had a flair for the grand response, so a few months into our relationship I quit my job, bought an around-the-world plane ticket, and went traveling for a year.

"It sucked for me," Amanda said.

There are only a handful of people you ever develop a strong romantic connection to, and having two of them sitting with me at the same table was powerfully strange. In some ways they seemed so similar: funny and smart and strongly opinionated. Most of the women I had liked shared those traits. But I saw the subtle ways Amanda was a bit sharper and harsher, how she leaned on jokes more heavily. Her energy bubbled with even greater sweetness than Jill's—*everything* was an ALL CAPS laugh—but it was a sweetness that only tasted good for so long, and eventually you noticed that half the jokes were at your expense.

In my telling, the time with Amanda was pretty straightforward: We dated for a while and it was great, but then I ran away. For her it was something quite different.

"It was very on and off," she said. "It was pretty intense at first, but you were always reluctant to put a definition on it. Then you decided to go around the world to be free but still sent romantic letters and love songs to screw with me. And that went on for a long time."

It came as a genuine surprise that almost ten years later, pregnant and married, she still seemed upset about those times we kept in touch after our relationship was over. "We saw each other maybe five days a year," I said, "and I assumed the other three hundred sixty days you weren't worried about us."

"Maybe it's the difference between men and women or our personal dynamic, but it wasn't like we would meet up and have an ice cream sundae. We would hook up and you would say intense things and then disappear."

That was true, I did do that. And not just with Amanda. For most of my twenties, whenever I met a girl I liked, the first thing I did was make very clear I wasn't interested in dating seriously. I would say the words: "We're never going to be a serious couple." But then I'd want to bake cookies and hold hands and watch a movie on the couch.

Whoever I was dating would agree to this insane bargain for a few months. Then she'd finally make some demands and I'd walk away. I somehow never quite appreciated how painful that was for the women on the other side of it. I went through those years pretty emotionally detached and probably didn't believe they really wanted to be with me anyway.

But even at the time I was aware enough to see the pattern and understand the basic cause: The attention of women was very important to me, too important to settle for the affection of only one.

The flaky, cheating, noncommittal man is society's unredeemable villain; so guys rarely talk about this stuff, even to each other. But after a few drinks one night a friend started poking around these ideas. He had recently broken up with his long-term live-in girlfriend and was having trouble working up the confidence to believe he could be faithful to someone else. He'd lost his virginity fifteen years before, but had devised a novel approach to commitment with his new girl-friend: He would wait until they were married to have sex.

"That doesn't make any sense," I said. "You're just waiting until you get married to deal with this stuff."

"Yeah, I guess so," he conceded. But this was the kind of nonsense men were ready to resort to in their clumsy, hapless desire to do right. Almost every guy I knew had some kind of technique. A friend in the music business stopped going to concerts without a chaperone. Another buddy put on fifty pounds after moving in with his girl-friend. A guy whose conscience wouldn't let him physically cheat told me he got his "fix" through nonstop flirting: "I mean, it isn't that satisfying, but it's something."

When I asked my friend Ryan for his method, he said he'd never come up with a good one: "I guess my technique is just to be tor-mented by temptation all the time and have it eventually destroy my relationship." And in the end, that was what a lot of guys did. Being committed sometimes felt like holding on to a rope as it lifted you off the ground and spun you in faster and faster circles. After Jill and I started dating, I hung on for as long as I could. When we broke up I felt the same disappointed relief I had when I bought that plane ticket to get away from Amanda. "Hell," Dostoyevsky wrote, "is the suffer-ing of being unable to love."

Sitting across from Amanda reminded me that my first marriage test had nothing to do with Jill. It was something I'd had to work out myself while we were apart. Doing that, moving past the drip-drip-drip need to see *if I could* had changed my life. It truly had. But it was far too late for Amanda.

JILL: "Is your husband anything like Brook?" I asked Amanda.

"No, not at all," she said. Amanda did not mince words, but I liked her. She was pretty, funny, and smart, three traits I hoped all of Brook's exes shared. Unlike Will and Brook, Amanda and I didn't look alike; she was significantly shorter, with straight dark brown hair that looked a lot more put together than my crazy curls. I guess Brook didn't have a physical "type."

But it was obvious she and Brook had known each other well.

Right off the bat she teased him about misplacing his keys. Brook was always losing something; I had found his AWOL wallet on the way out the door to meet Amanda. The two of them joked around but not like Will and I had. Their rapport had a much darker tone.

"No, my husband's not like Brook," she said. "From day one, I felt like I had to convince Brook that marriage is great and children are a good thing and Subarus are good cars. With my husband, we're on the same page; he wants the same things. And I think that marriage-wise, advice-wise, that is huge. You should be picturing the same thing. At all the little milestones along the way, you want to say, 'Look, we bought our first gardening tool,' and both be excited about it."

Amanda almost seemed to relish the chance to get this old resentment off her chest. Brook mainly sat there and took the punishment; she had earned her arrows. But it was hard for me to hear so many familiar complaints; I recognized the guy she was describing. I had met Brook not long after he returned from that around-the-world trip and he was a charming, disappointing guy to date. He would seem totally invested in me one minute and then disappear the next.

But my strongest emotional reaction to Amanda's stories was sadness. Brook had spent his entire twenties in this awful cycle of hurting not only the people he cared about but himself as well.

More than a few women I knew dated guys in similar cycles and, like Amanda, thought they could "convince" them to commit. But a proposal from someone who wasn't truly ready was much worse than no proposal at all; it was a poisoned prize. Trying to convince a guy to marry you was like trying to convince a pair of shoes to fit. All these years later, Amanda still looked at Brook and felt blisters. And that was her right; at least she was honest about it and had moved on with her life.

Because painful breakups really only offer two paths forward:

move on or forgive. The problem is that a lot of people delude themselves into thinking they've forgiven. Then they end up reconnecting with the person who's hurt them and ultimately can't help but rehash old pain. I'd always been a firm believer that if you decide to reconcile, then you really need to forgive. Not just say, "I accept your apology." Not just agree to get back together. But really forgive and resolve that what happened in the past will stay there. Lunch with Amanda was a test of whether I'd actually done that—or whether the anger she showed on the surface I still kept deep down.

"We've done a bit of Brook-bashing today, which is interesting for me." I had to fight back some tears. "But who Brook was at twenty-five is not who he is now."

Amanda kind of nodded. I couldn't tell if she agreed with me or pitied me for thinking Brook could ever change. But I didn't need her agreement. It didn't matter if she was able to see the nurturing, reliable, emotionally open man sitting next to her. The Brook I lived with and told my secrets to was a man I trusted. Sitting down with Amanda only made our growth more noticeable.

My head was pretty foggy when we said good-bye and started walking home. Lost in my thoughts, I barely noticed when Brook diverted us to Macy's. After some aimless browsing, I saw him staring at me with a really weird look on his face.

"Today has me thinking," he said. "I'd like to get your finger sized." Through some really nervous laughter I said, "Yeah . . . sure." And a few minutes later we watched a size seven loop slip onto my shaking hand.

Money

DATE #4

Trading Credit Cards

BROOK: It was a perfect October afternoon, so I hopped on my bike and pedaled down Fifteenth Street, past the White House and the Washington Monument all the way to East Potomac Park. One great thing about living in D.C. is that you can easily bike to a public golf course. I went to the clubhouse and pulled Jill's Visa from my wallet. She wasn't just paying for my round of golf; everything each of us bought for the next month would be paid for with the other person's money.

Now that we had established a healthy degree of trust, we could start testing the kinds of issues married couples face but that we had long avoided. We decided to start with money, in part because so many relationship researchers said it was the unsexy key to a happy marriage, and in part because we believed it would be easy. We were so well suited on money stuff, we thought. Jill and I already shared a credit card for joint expenses like groceries and the Internet bill. And we had agreed without much discussion to combine all our bank accounts if we ever tied the knot—it seemed like the obvious choice. Exchanging credit cards for a month . . . How hard could that be?

But as we discussed our *Money* dates with friends, something strange happened, something that suggested we might not quite understand what we were in for. They kept telling these bizarre-sounding stories about the ways married couples deal with money. One friend described the elaborate hoops her parents had jumped through to maintain independent finances: separate car payments and divided savings, their own groceries and their own furniture. When kids came along, the couple took things to their logical conclusion— Dad paid for the son, Mom was responsible for the daughter, our friend. But Dad made most of the money, so that was bad news for our friend. She never had toys or clothes or an education quite as nice as her brother. That was batshit crazy, right? Marriage meant you were in the same boat, emotionally and financially. Why pretend to have separate money when it's really all part of the same big pot? It seemed incredibly obvious until I put Jill's Visa in my wallet. Suddenly, the simple mechanics of moving through the world became a constant morality play. Six dollars at the dry cleaners; $4.82 for coffee—every swipe somehow felt *wrong.* And it wasn't the credit card fraud that made me nervous (I was never asked for ID), it was something more personal. Just by living my life, it felt like I was taking something that belonged to Jill.

It only got worse when the charges were bigger and less necessary. On day twelve of the credit card swap I spent $63 on a friend's dinner, the next day $118 for a coat. These were purchases I'd normally make and could definitely afford, but it didn't feel quite right to have Jill pay for them. On poker night, her cash bought my chips and I lost $46 of her hard-earned coin. Was that fair? Did it mean she should have a say in how I spent my money? Did it mean I shouldn't play poker?

I slowly understood that combining your finances creates a 24/7 tether to your partner. You might go alone to work and then get drinks with friends, but if the money you earn and spend is shared with someone else, you're never quite alone. Joining your money means losing a fundamental type of independence.

The meaning of that crystalized in one purchase. As Jill's birthday approached I started shopping for a gift. At first I didn't understand what that meant. But when I finally had pictures of our recent trip to Europe framed, I realized I couldn't buy them for her. She paid the $150 herself.

In a sense, marrying our money would mean we'd never buy each other another gift. That piece of jewelry or weekend getaway isn't truly a present if the person you give it to pays for half. So maybe separate pots of cash did make sense. Then the choice of how you spent that money—on diamond earrings instead of new golf clubs—had some real meaning. But should the golf clubs really come from a separate pot? What about the new winter jacket? What about the coffee? Where did it end? How did you draw that line?

The difficulty of the question helped explain why so many couples resorted to elaborate strategies for keeping financial separation. But there also seemed to be something else at work, something about the unspoken way money represented power in a relationship. After five years of marriage, our close friends Bill and Josey shared a mortgage and two sons, but not a bank account. "I've suggested we collapse the savings accounts into one," Bill said. "But she, for some kind of peace of mind, wants it separate. She wants to know how much she accumulates over time." All of their accounts were still linked into one online login so Bill could just look through the charges at the end of the month. Josey knew he did that so she would tell him if she was going to make a big purchase. "She doesn't want me to be surprised," Bill said.

"And do you tell Josey before you make a big purchase?"

"Honestly, I don't feel like I have to check with her," Bill said. "It's a bit of a double standard, but I make more and I manage the finances."

And there it was, the thing no one wanted to say: If we both made and both spent the same amount, this would be easy, but of course we don't. And Bill was essentially saying that the partner who makes less is supposed to be more careful about what they spend. At the moment, in my relationship, that was me. I had left my job at the *Washington Post* the month before and returned to freelancing out of our apartment. I was hoping to score a bigger job as a network TV correspondent, and in the meantime I could bike down to the golf course at East Potomac Park while Jill did her consulting work in an office across the river.

Jill was winning most of our bread, and we both said we were okay with that. One of us might do better at work or stay home to take care of the kids, but it would be *our* money, right? I'd always assumed so. But I started to wonder if equally sharing money was one of those partnership fantasies, like an open marriage or evenly divided newborn feedings—a simple-sounding solution that would never quite work.

JILL: I didn't make a purchase as Brook Silva-Braga until day three of our credit card swap. I guess I just assumed I was going to spend way more than him, so I wanted to minimize as best I could. That after-noon I couldn't hold out any longer; I was starving and needed a snack. My heart swelled with pride as my hand grasped a cup of Joe's Discount Yogurt, half the price of the delicious fancy Greek yogurt I preferred. I was saving Brook money right off the bat! What a girlfriend!

I'd always considered Brook and me to be very much in sync about money; I couldn't recall a single time we'd fought about it. We shared the same mind-set: Money was the thing that allowed us to have the comforts and experiences that were important to us, but it wasn't something to live our lives for.

A lot of guys talked a good game about prioritizing life goals over making more money, but would they really turn down a pro-motion if it meant seeing their kids less? Probably not. But I would, and I hoped my husband would too. I'd recently left a higher-paying job for one with more rewarding work and less frequent travel. And in making that choice for myself, I discovered that I wanted a part-ner who was willing to at least consider such trade-offs as well.

Brook was almost militant in his refusal to pursue money for its own sake. Before we met, he'd left a very desirable job with HBO to travel and make independent documentaries. And the gamble had paid off; he managed to sell his first film to MTV. I always found Brook's fiercely independent spirit really attractive, and it came with an added bonus: unlike all the other "creative types" I'd dated, Brook's risks were calculated and tended to work out.

But as I got to know him, I learned the real secret to his life of adventure: Brook was ... let's not say cheap, but ... *extremely efficient* with his money. He'd eat $2 Mamoun's falafels and $2.50 Zaragoza tacos night after night and then use the savings to fund a five-month backpacking trip across Africa. A taxi was a luxury reserved for, well, pretty much when someone else was paying. I'm sure his creative budgeting turned off a lot of women, but I wasn't looking for a sugar daddy. I had just moved to Manhattan on an entry-level salary, so I was also in the market for $2 cans of beer and Brook seemed to know where all of them were hiding.

We had great fun scrimping together back then, and used our generally frugal lifestyle to fund a handful of luxuries we really cared about. We became the couple who happily backpacked across China on $20 a day, eating street food and sleeping on floors, then came home and splurged on a giant TV. Those decisions were somehow effortless; our tastes and priorities just naturally matched in this idiosyncratic way.

But in our day-to-day lives we still maintained a lot of financial privacy—I didn't see the receipts for his camera equipment or share the cost of every outfit I bought. Revealing all those life expenses made me a bit nervous. I wasn't so sure Brook understood what it cost me to stay properly fed and dressed, and I wasn't sure I wanted him to.

After a few days of shitty-yogurt consumption, I realized my belt-tightening made no sense. We all have unavoidable expenses, and gaming the credit card swap ignored the whole point of the exercise, which was to spend honestly and see what conversations that prompted later.

When I stopped trying to impress him with how little money I needed to survive, the swap got interesting. Twenty-seven dollars to pay off old toll charges. A $15 taxi when I accidentally bought more groceries than I could carry. Fifty bucks for dinner with a friend. I was spending like I typically would, but something felt different. Before every purchase I thought about whether I was being wasteful.

I almost always went through with it, but knowing it wasn't my money made me stop and think.

When we conceived of Date #4, I hadn't worried about Brook using my credit card. I trusted that he would spend sensibly, as he always had. So my jaw hit the floor when we tallied our expenses. Brook spent nearly twice as much as I had! He'd used my Visa to buy a custom suit, two winter coats, Amtrak train tickets, and roughly a million rounds of golf. (Turns out golf is an expensive hobby.) Brook insisted the suit had been an incredible deal, and I'm certain it was. But it was a "deal" that helped him spend 100 percent more than me!

The charges themselves might not have bothered me, but Brook has a special character trait that made his swipes more complicated: He loses *everything*. His keys, his glasses, a cup of water. It was mainly funny and sometimes I even liked it because I was good at finding his stuff so I got to play the hero—"Your glasses are on the kitchen table, dear."

But it wasn't so funny when it was my money getting wasted on lost items right and left. Before this date, I didn't have any personal stake in how he treated his things. But that $35 umbrella (three times as expensive as mine!) he bought with my card and lost the *very next day*? That was annoying. And since it was unlikely Brook would ever get better at keeping track of his things, this date had me worried I'd come to resent constantly replacing his stuff if our money was merged.

By the end of our monthlong credit card swap I was humbled by how tough it was to completely share money, even for two people who seemed to be so in sync. Money was the most concrete representation of the choices we made in life—the things we did to make money, and ways we chose to spend it. Pooling your money with another person meant revealing and ultimately funding those choices. It felt weird to know Brook would see how, when, and where I made a purchase—and by extension be aware of all the decisions I made. Did I really want him to know about every last beauty treatment, snack, or gift I ever bought? Maybe all those couples with separate accounts knew something we were just starting to learn.

"Part of what makes it possible to be married and accept that you're going to be with someone forever is knowing that you haven't given up everything you are to become a part of a couple," our friend Tom said one night over beers. His wife paid the mortgage, he paid the kids' tuition. But Tom explained his reasons for the arrangement in a way I hadn't heard before, in a way that didn't even have that much to do with money.

"I wanted to get married. I am married. I'm happily . . ." He paused for a moment, as if to fact-check himself. "I'm as happily married as anybody is. But sometimes you don't want to be part of a unit, you want to be your own person. And I think with finances that's not a harmful thing. It gives me a semblance of independence to keep my money separate."

It was a bit of a shock to almost agree with him. I'd always thought—to the extent I bothered to think about it—that shared finances were the standard postwedding setup. It was the model I'd seen my parents and brother use. I assumed we'd follow their lead and I expected these *Money* dates to be a cakewalk, but it turns out if something gives a lot of couples trouble, chances are it will give you trouble too. The last month had me questioning how to balance our individual privacy with the reality that when you're married, ultimately, so is your money.

When we handed back our credit cards, I was more confused about the whole thing than I had been when we started.

DATE #5

Budget Crunch

JILL: Financial clarity did not magically arrive with the start of our fifth date—perhaps because we began the next month's experiment with total disrespect for the challenge. The idea was to cut our spending in half, testing how our relationship dealt with a much tighter budget. But we had a *whole month* to get our expenses down, so we could splurge a little at the beginning, right? Friends in New York were hosting a cocktail party, so I reached for a box on the top shelf of the whiskey aisle and pulled down a $50 bottle of Scotch; more than my entire budget for the day. *We'll scrimp later*, I promised myself.

Like toys and life rafts, money isn't that hard to share when there's plenty of it. I remembered sitting at a fancy New York restaurant some years before as a husband at the next table explained to his wife that her spending was unsustainable. For the rest of the meal they played out the worst clichés of an Upper East Side couple. She hadn't married him for his looks, she said, and now he was holding back on money too. He understood that her salon visits and trainer sessions were also for his benefit, but their giant mortgage had to be a priority.

That was back when Brook and I had just started dating, and the spoiled couple's spat seemed absurd to me at the time. I was still in that terribly paid PR job and Brook was in his struggling-filmmaker phase. My work was paying for the fancy dinner, but Brook and I filled most nights with those $2.50 tacos from Zaragoza—I lived right upstairs in an apartment so small you could extend your arms in the living room and touch both walls; we dubbed it the "gastric bypass apartment." Now, five years later, we could afford to take a taxi back to an apartment where seven people could congregate without violating the fire code. And this new lifestyle made me wonder: Had we unknowingly become more like that spoiled couple, able to buy our way out of disagreements, for now?

Before we could test the impact of rationing our money, we had to calculate what our "normal" spending was, and that became its own challenge. With great trepidation I summed my expenses from the last year and divided by twelve to get a monthly average. Yikes. I was careful with my money but had never added it up like this and was shocked how much still went to things like booze and dinners out. Brook and I might travel cheap, but I'd still spent an ungodly amount just in the last year on plane tickets to California, Montreal, and Colorado. Those trips were such fun, but I realized I'd been in denial about the costs—our $20-a-day jaunts were in the past. Brook tallied his own monthly average, added it to mine, and cut the total in half. "Time to get thrifty!" we exclaimed.

And then we immediately—and I do mean immediately—blew the budget. It wasn't just the bottle of whiskey but a lot of other New York trip costs: a rental car and gas, dinners and beers. We basically ignored the date and assumed we'd tighten the belt when we got back home.

In the first week we spent 50 percent more than we were supposed to. So we fired up the college diet and started cooking a lot of pasta. I ate the leftovers for lunch. Brook rediscovered his appreciation for cheap beer. We stayed in a lot. If it had been summertime, we could have ridden our bikes to a museum or grabbed our gloves and played catch in the park. But no, we were budget crunching during a particularly cold November and with bars and restaurants off limits we almost never left the house!

I wish I could say I used this challenge to develop some wallet-friendly hobbies or work out a ton. But no, mostly I just sulked, then felt guilty for sulking. And then I felt the sulking become something much darker. I could tell I was tiptoeing toward depression.

"There's nothing to eat," Brook said as I got home from work one night.

"Well, I went grocery shopping the last five times so it's your turn," I said. We weren't arguing about money, but our days were increasingly filled with these tense interactions. We were both on edge, and I couldn't tell if it was my bad mood that had started it or if he had found his own road to Sad City. I waited for it to wear off, but as the days went by our conversations remained sour. It was the rockiest time we'd had since getting back together.

After a week of tension, I finally brought it up. "Brook, I feel like we're fighting a lot all of a sudden. Is there something that's bothering you that we should talk about?" I waited for him to answer.

"No, everything's fine," he finally said with a shrug and a blank look. *Ugh, everything's not fine.* It was lousy and familiar.

Back when we were first dating there were a lot of times when something (or someone) was irritating one of us and we would silently stew rather than bring it up. Brook seemed especially incapable of starting tough conversations, but I was only marginally better. I think we were both afraid of hurting the other's feelings, so we just kept quiet as things got worse and worse. After reuniting we'd mostly managed to avoid those ruts, but here we were again.

I could feel a tightness in my heart and in my gut, and just like old times I spent a lot of energy fixating on this feeling. It genuinely scared me. It felt like backsliding.

Of course, fixating on what seemed wrong didn't fix it. So I decided to try something more proactive. I would keep track of all the times we were unable to talk openly about the difficult things our dates brought up. And while I was at it, I'd also catalog any other major issues that arose. I wasn't worried about annoyances, like bickering when we cooked together, but rather fundamental incompatibilities— things that might cause serious difficulty over the long term, even after decades together. So I started building what I called the Fifty Years In List (FYI List for short) to collect whatever red flags I found as we went through these dates.

The point wasn't to keep track of fights. Fights I expected; conflict wasn't a reason not to get married. I was looking for the big stuff a fight couldn't resolve: reasons I might ultimately regret marrying Brook.

The first entry on my FYI List: *Being honest about what's bothering us.* I wasn't ready to sign up for a life of guessing what was on Brook's mind or holding in my own emotions; we'd already tried that unsuccessfully the first time we dated. I didn't write anything about money on the FYI List even though that was what this date was meant to test. The tight budget seemed to be more of a setting for the fight than its true cause.

I wasn't ready to tell Brook about my FYI List. I figured I'd keep it to myself until I had more to say about it. I hoped the list would be short, but our bad moods had me fearing I might fill a few more pages of my notebook as we stressed our relationship across the remaining dates.

BROOK: Toward the end of the month, another group of friends invited us to a party. There was definitely no money left for a $50 bottle of whiskey. I surveyed our barren liquor shelf, hoping we had an extra bottle of something hiding in the back. The month had emptied our cabinets and cleaned out our fridge.

Not that it should have mattered. Our lowly first years together had been a nonstop adventure. Being young and broke in New York was like writing a haiku; the constraints inspired creativity that led to small, beautiful moments—the unpredictable fun on a 3 A.M. subway ride, the joy of discovery at a hole-in-the-wall dumpling spot.

But in the years since, we had stopped pinching pennies. We now paid more in rent than we'd spent backpacking together across Africa and Asia. I had hoped the budget crunch would inspire some of that old joie de vivre. It hadn't. Rather than getting ready for the party, Jill was sitting silently on the couch. That wasn't a good sign; unless she was in a movie theater or a deep sleep, Jill was pretty much never quiet.

"Brook, can I talk to you about something?" she said. As I walked over I saw tears spilling down her cheeks. "I feel like we aren't enjoying each other's company these days and are really annoyed with each other," she said. "But I don't know what's going on."

It was that last part that seemed the scariest—the fact we didn't really understand what was wrong and didn't have the words to express what we felt. She wanted me to explain why we were fighting yet didn't have an explanation herself. Were we really in crisis over too many pasta dinners? I didn't think so, but I couldn't really say what it was about. So I fixed the thing I could and found a way to get us out of the house.

I walked back over to the liquor shelf and found a half-full bottle of vodka in the back. I brought it to the kitchen sink and filled it to the top with water, giggling almost uncontrollably. Jill was laughing too, wiping her eyes with the wrist of her sweater. We put on our heaviest coats and walked up to the party with our bottle of Absolut Tap. When we got there the beer was warm and the snacks mostly gone, but it felt good just to be out.

At the ragged, drunken end of the night someone convinced their friends to do a round of shots and pointed at our bottle of vodka. I cringed as Jill played cocktail waitress and filled their glasses with half a measure of hydrogen and oxygen.

"Salud!"

They seemed impressed with how mild it tasted and asked for another round. I took it as 100-proof evidence that half a bottle of vodka could still be more fun than a full bottle of Scotch. It didn't solve what we had to fix, but it reminded me why we'd made it this far.

DATE #6

Full Dicloure

BROOK: The next morning I dug out our waffle iron and defrosted some blueberries; if Jill ever lost her taste for fruit waffles I'd have no reliable way to improve her mood. We ate with our laptops in front of us and, in a row of browser tabs across the tops of our screens, we pulled up every bank account, retirement statement, credit card bill, and student loan balance associated with our social security numbers. For years we'd hinted at what was in these accounts but never actually talked numbers. Now we would share everything. Half a dozen windows on each of our computers contained a record of every dollar we had saved or borrowed.

It only took one story to convince us to do this date. It came from our friend Grace, whose sister Sarah had met a guy at a party and soon found herself in a serious relationship: her toothbrush in his bathroom, his work clothes in her closest. Finally they moved in together.

"So the guy proposes to her," Grace said. "But all this time Sarah has somehow managed to hide from him this immense amount of debt. Student loans, maxed-out credit cards, she's like one step from bankruptcy but she's afraid to tell him. And the wedding day is getting closer and closer. So finally our mom says to her, 'You have to tell him or I'm going to tell him for you.'"

Sarah's case was extreme, but it was easy to see how it happened: there's something embarrassing about yourself you're never quite motivated to mention, you're afraid it will scare them off, you're certain you can change before it matters. I'm sure it also happens with stuff other than money, but no one is forced into bankruptcy through messy closets or a sports obsession. If we were going to follow through on our plans to join our finances, we needed to know what we'd actually be combining.

You might think we had a lot of money. Neither of us carried a credit card balance; Jill had a high-paying business job. But as we totaled our balances, the picture wasn't so rosy. It started with Jill's business school loans. A big reason she made so much money was her degree from Columbia Business School, but the cost was massive—$150,000 for the two-year program. When we added up the totals in her checking and savings accounts, they were eclipsed by what she still owed in loans—Jill had a negative net worth.

That didn't surprise or bother me—I had always supported the high-priced degree as a good long-term investment—but it did put a bit of pressure on my half of the balance sheet. On the plus side, I had no debt and some savings. And my old documentaries still generated enough income to cover my share of rent. But since leaving the nine-to-five job I'd been mostly living off my savings, which were starting to shrink rather noticeably. We totaled my accounts and Jill looked confused.

"So wait . . . Brook . . . you have no money."

"Well, there's a little bit of money."

"Yeah, but I thought there was more." A deep breath. "Okay."

JILL: Our nest egg belonged to a sparrow. The number at the bottom of our Excel spreadsheet made an impressive SAT score but was an embarrassing net worth for two thirty-somethings. Fuck. I'd just somehow deluded myself into assuming there was more savings between us. *Sure, I don't have any money, but Brook must!*

As he did with most bad news, Brook took the meager bottom line in stride. It took me longer to process disappointing news.

"We're in our thirties and our savings couldn't buy a '94 Corolla," I said.

"Yes, and . . ." Brook responded. *Yes, and* was a little piece of relationship magic we had stumbled on months before. It was stolen from improv comics who were trained never to say *No*, but instead answer with, *Yes, and*. We used it the same way, fully aware it was 30 percent ridiculous, and it somehow worked. When I heard *Yes, and* . . . I knew Brook was really disagreeing with me, but it still softened his words and made me feel heard.

"Yes, and . . . we're both healthy people with useful skills," he said. "Even if it means doing some job we hate, we'll always find a way to get by." He was right; we weren't going to end up on the streets.

The very fact that we were able to calculate our financial situation so precisely was its own silver lining. I couldn't help but be impressed by the detailed cash flow spreadsheet Brook shared. He seemed to have maintained it for years. As the daughter of not one but two accountants, I found that it took on almost erotic properties. "Oh, so you've been tracking your spend versus savings burn rate since 2006," I noted breathlessly. "Your 401(k)s have all been rolled over to a single IRA?" I had to fan myself. Even if he wasn't the most organized guy in general, this date proved that Brook meticulously managed his finances . . . and I really liked that.

Opening up our books felt like a big relationship moment. It didn't directly answer that item on my FYI List about *Being honest about what's bothering us*, but it showed that we could expose something personal and grow closer rather than more distant. And it allowed me to think more concretely about how we might manage accounts with both of our names on them.

At the start of these dates, Brook and I had both been strongly in the camp of joining our money, but we now appreciated why so many well-adjusted couples decided to keep some financial separation even when they joined their lives. Toward the end of the *Money* dates, I chatted with my colleague Landers about the dilemma. Single and twenty-three, he came to the question fresh.

"So if you get married, would you want to keep your and your wife's money separate?" I asked.

"No, definitely not. It should just be in one pool together."

"That's what I thought too!" I said, and then listed some of the reasons—privacy, gift giving, independence, simplicity—couples cited when maintaining separate accounts.

"Yeah . . . but . . . what about the feeling?" The *feeling*? This bachelor was talking feelings! "Like, what does that separation say? You're marrying someone, you're sharing a bed, a life, a kitchen . . . and not your money? If I get married I want to share everything."

I'd been searching for a simple way to explain why I still felt joint finances were right for Brook and me, but it was a dude born in the 1990s and on his way to a Tinder date who said it best.

I wanted to *feel* our union and have it change my life. I'd had roommates since I turned eighteen. I didn't want my husband to be just another person I divided up bills with. I wanted to plan and experience our lives together, and money was both a symbol and embodiment of that.

There was one final step in our "Full Dicloure," something we'd been building up to for months: a credit score showdown. And we weren't just getting our scores out of curiosity, there was a grand prize at stake—we agreed that if we ever got married, whoever had the higher score would have final say over the wedding budget.

With our computers side by side, we logged on to myFICO.com and each paid $15 to see our scores for the first time. I was thrilled with my 817, and even more excited for Brook's 802. We were both creditworthy (I mean, who could doubt a U.S. financial institution's opinion on creditworthiness?), and I would have final fiscal say on the ceremony if we made it through the next thirty-four dates!

Kids

DATE #7

Borrowing a Baby

JILL: Our alarm went off at 10:30 A.M. on a Saturday and I sat up with a cloudy head and gummy mouth after a night of cocktails, dinner, wine, and more cocktails. Our apartment looked more like a frat house than a nursery; cigar ash perfumed the living room. And in less than ninety minutes our friends' nine-month-old son, Jack, would arrive for twenty-four hours in our care. We started cleaning. And I started wondering just how fast I could truly get my life together.

That question had been nagging at me for two weeks, since my last annual lady doctor visit. After finishing the routine exam, my gynecologist removed his gloves and gave me a serious look. "When you're dressed, why don't you come to my office?" I fumbled out of the cold stirrups. What did he just say? It didn't sound like *Everything looks good, see you in a year.* What was wrong?

"Earlier you mentioned your boyfriend," my doctor began. We were now sitting in his wood-paneled office surrounded by framed evidence that he knew more than me. My chair felt absurdly far away from his massive, tidy desk. "Are you two serious?"

"Yeah," I replied. "We're talking more and more about marriage these days." I told him about our forty dates.

"Have you discussed children?" he pressed. It was getting awkward.

"Umm, kind of. Like I think we both want kids down the line."

"Yes, well, I think it's important for you to start thinking about that more seriously. The sooner you start trying to get pregnant, the better. The longer you wait, the more likely you'll have trouble conceiving." Ouch. I wasn't *that* old. I reassured him it wouldn't be a problem. My mom had my sister when she was thirty-nine, I said. That doesn't mean much, he said.

"So, when you say sooner . . . you mean like, within a few years I should start trying?"

He gave me a stern but kind look. "No. Sooner as in 'as soon as possible.'" I was unmarried on the wrong side of thirty, so I probably should have seen this coming. But honestly the intervention was a complete surprise, I just didn't feel that old. My life didn't seem all that different than my life in college. When a friend confided in me she was pregnant, I still wasn't sure whether to say, "I'm so happy for you!" or "Oh my God, what are you going to do?" Actually *trying* to get preggers was a foreign, grown-up thing I'd worry about when I was ready to move on from the cocktails-and-cigars phase. My doctor suggested an entirely different schedule.

By some hangover miracle, our apartment was ready when Jack and his parents pulled up in their Subaru. The next few minutes were like unpacking a clown car. There was a stroller, collapsible crib, diaper bag, food, toys, clothes, a tablet computer, and books (seemingly meant to be read, but actually to chew). And right next to the pile, a plump, adorable baby boy. Jack's parents didn't have any family nearby and seemed eager for some free time (their plan, according to Dad: "drinking and fornicating"). We were soon on our own with one happy baby and—I'm not kidding—a detailed Power-Point instruction manual titled "The Definitive Guide to Baby Jack."

I wasn't nervous about taking care of Jack. I had two young nieces so I was pretty comfortable feeding, changing, burping, and soothing little ones. But Brook and I had never been alone with a child. I had no idea how he'd do as a dad.

There was a lot riding on both Brook's parenting skills and our ability to make this relationship work. If Brook and I passed this forty-date test, the future was relatively easy to picture. He'd be my diaper-changing, Little League–coaching, parent-teacher-conferencing partner sooner rather than later.

But what if we didn't pass the test? I pictured a painful breakup and then calculated the long journey to motherhood from there: time to heal from the split, then finding a promising partner, dating, getting married, and only then trying to get pregnant. When I thought about it that way, being single in my midthirties sounded terrifying. My gut reaction to the doctor's visit had been, "I'm not ready to be a mom," but in the last couple of weeks I'd started to accept that if I ever wanted kids, I needed to be honest about the realities of babymaking as I got older. Worrying about finding the *perfect* partner felt a little foolish. *Good enough* suddenly seemed semi-sensible.

It was infuriating to even think about "settling." Brook and other men would never face that kind of compromise. A doctor would never pull them aside to trumpet the dying days of their fertility! I tried balancing my doctor's warning with the stories of women I'd seen settle for so-so men and end up in shitty relationships. If I didn't find a great partner, did I really want to raise a family alone or with someone who wasn't a true match? Probably not. So, maybe kids wouldn't be a part of my future if it didn't work out with Brook. No pressure!

Baby Jack didn't appear troubled by the heavy stakes of our time together. He was a happy little guy as we all played on the floor and got prepped for lunch. It was *so* sweet to see Brook take care of a wee one. He didn't seem awkward at all, and if he wasn't sure about something he'd ask me or consult "The Definitive Guide to Baby Jack."

At lunchtime, we plopped Jack in his green plastic chair and watched him gum some steamed carrots and hard-boiled eggs. Maybe we forgot the bib, and yeah, he was spitting out more than he was eating, but we were being parents! Our baby seemed happy! A warm sensation washed over me as I allowed myself to pretend for a moment that Jack was ours and this was a normal Saturday for our cute little family.

Things seemed to be under control, so I left the boys to finish lunch and ran downstairs to change the laundry. When I returned to our floor and heard muffled baby cries, I realized one of our neighbors also had a . . . oh wait, it was our baby crying! I opened the door to see Jack *screaming* as Brook desperately corralled him on the couch trying to change his diaper.

"Oh, no, what happened?"

"I don't know, he was fine . . . and then he wasn't fine," Brook said. "I thought maybe he needed a fresh diaper." The new diaper had not exactly been secured in the traditional manner—it looked a bit like a piece of IKEA furniture assembled without the instructions. Jack kept wailing.

"Here, let me." I grabbed Jack and began to deploy some tried-and-true aunt tricks. Bouncing, cooing, toys, food. But nothing helped.

Fifteen minutes of bawling, then twenty-five. As Jack struggled to take in enough air to support his desperate screams, I started to wonder if we should call his parents. We were running out of ideas. It wasn't recommended by "The Definitive Guide," but Brook mixed up a warm bottle and brought it over. And Jack latched on for dear life. Total quiet. The bottle's nipple leaked and the formula wasn't quite dissolved, but it worked. The three of us finally exhaled.

BROOK: When Jack cried uncontrollably I had this deep, unsettling feeling of helplessness. And when that bottle finally made him stop, I experienced waves of paternal, humanity-affirming victory. I had solved Jack's riddle!

I noticed a long time ago that we can't objectively describe the people who are closest to us—I can't hear my mom's accent or really tell how pretty my girlfriend is. My impressions are too colored by my feelings for them. By Sunday morning I already felt that way about Jack.

He wasn't a cute kid or an ugly kid—he was just *Jack*, the little guy who laughed when I flew his stuffed animals around the room, cried when I put him down for a nap, and bit the wrong part of the teething ring no matter how many times I put the right part in his mouth. It was weird to feel so connected to someone I'd just met and couldn't talk to. When his parents said they were coming to pick Jack up, we actually asked them to wait a bit so we could hang out with him a while longer.

Probably more than any other date, borrowing the baby gave me a sense of our future—what having a family with Jill would be like. For the most part it felt really good. Jill had amazing motherly instincts, and our time with Jack confirmed she'd be a great parent.

But she could also be a condescending one. Jill definitely thought she knew best and offered only begrudging approval of my efforts.

It was me, after all, who had finally gotten Jack to stop crying. But Jill didn't dwell on that point; I wasn't sure she even really noticed. I imagine having a baby would be intense and humbling, a time of constant discovery and frequent mistakes. But parental humility seemed like a dangerous admission in front of Jill, who was so anxious to be the expert. My biggest concern going into and coming out of this date was that she would treat me as a less-than-equal parent.

When I mentioned this concern to Jill, she was not especially receptive. "If you felt I was condescending, I think that says more about your insecurities around babies than how I behaved," she said.

But there was no time for Mommy and Daddy to fight. We were heading outside for breakfast. First, we needed to get Jack in the stroller—sounds easy enough. But some kind of hidden lock jammed the wheels and as we took turns tugging and twisting, two tires fell right off. (My lawyer advises me not to comment on whether Jack was in the stroller at the time.)

We finally stepped into the cold, sunny morning and passed another stroller-pushing mom whose baby was much, much more bundled up than poor Jack. We averted our eyes, considered our options, and then piled Jack's spare clothes on his lap as a makeshift blanket. Time was of the essence. We needed to find breakfast before the cold breached his pile of laundry, but the stroller couldn't fit into the little coffee shop by our house and all of the brunch places near P Street were already too crowded. Jill started hurrying north: "That taqueria just off Fourteenth Street!"

Finding breakfast was a big deal for Jill because she hoped (maybe a little too optimistically) that raising kids didn't have to spoil your social life. *See, you can still go out and get breakfast on a Sunday morning!* We walked in and it looked perfect—big, empty, and casual. And then just a moment later another stroller rolled in. And then two more. It turned out breakfast tacos weren't just a good neighborhood choice, they were seemingly the only choice for a couple with a baby in tow. Jill slumped in her seat.

"When I've pictured my life as a mom I've always assumed I would still get out a lot," she said slowly, scanning the baby parade. "I figured if you're cool enough and patient enough you can wheel a stroller into a coffee shop or even a beer hall or concert venue."

She looked at Jack, who remained unmoved by her existential crisis. "You've taught me that maybe there are only a few spots that work for a family. Maybe this will be a bigger adjustment than I'd like to admit." Jill poked his round belly and sighed. "But you're still really cute!"

We strolled back down Fourteenth Street and met Jack's parents outside our building. Good-byes over, Jill and I sprawled across the couch and watched football to recover.

DATE #8

Sounds Like a Newborn

BROOK: A few nights later, as we were starting another *Kids* date, I had a strange, awful dream. I was on the side of the road in the middle of a desert changing my clothes and when I got the shirt up over my head, all my video equipment was gone. I ran after the thief and came upon a shoot-out between rival African warlords and found Jill, bound at the wrists and screaming, being carried away onto a roof I couldn't reach.

I was jarred from my nightmare a few minutes after 1 A.M. by my phone's alarm. But in a way, waking up only made the dream more real. Date #8 was about losing some of the things I cared about most—a focus on my career, quality time with Jill—in the service of raising a child. If my dream was any indication, just simulating the sacrifice already had me troubled. Was I really ready to be a dad?

Before bed that night, we found a random alarm app and set it to ring three times between 11 P.M. and 8 A.M. We also put fourteen scraps of paper in a bowl, each slip describing a task we'd have to complete when the alarm went off during the night. It was our way of mimicking the exhausted stress of raising a newborn: never letting ourselves sleep for more than three hours straight for the next seven days. We needed a baby to take care of but didn't want to traumatize an actual child, so we adopted a twelve-pound watermelon and named her "Mel."

Some of the chores in the bowl were fairly easy: five minutes bouncing Mel, ten minutes stroking her beautiful green rind while swaddling her in a blanket. But then there was stuff that would keep us up half the night: cooking a meal, sweeping and mopping our floors, cleaning the cabinets. When we asked friends with children for suggestions, they mostly involved vomit, so at the end of some tasks we were required to take a shower. When the alarm woke me from my nightmare that first night, I put my hand in the bowl and pulled out the worst damn chore of all: "Do a full cycle of laundry." *Seriously?* I gathered some dirty clothes and took the elevator to the basement washing machine. I wasn't allowed to sleep while they spun, so I put on a pot of water for tea.

"Oh no," Jill rasped from the bedroom, "already resorting to caffeine."

If I was ready to be a dad, it was probably because of Jill. In some vague way I'd always assumed I wanted a family, but after I met Jill it became a much more specific picture. This might sound weird, but one of the first things I thought when we started hanging out years earlier was, "Jill is going to make a good mom." We weren't spending time with kids, or even talking about them, but when I looked at her, even though we barely knew each other, I couldn't help but picture her two decades older as the mother of my children. It was the strangest thing. I guess she just kind of oozed all the stuff I imagined a mother should be. She was fun. Responsible. Resilient. Smart. Caring.

Through all those lousy times when we first dated and I was filled with constant doubt, that vision of our future life was the most pressing reason to stay. The image was so vivid—four of us playing in the southern corner of Prospect Park; only the kids' faces were out of focus. Jill was smiling and I could just barely notice that her hair was gray—but it was hard to tell she was older because it was only now that she finally looked like the person I'd always imagined her being.

I took for granted that Jill shared this vision. For years she presented symptoms of low-grade baby fever that only intensified after she became an aunt. "I love my nieces sooooo much," she'd say after a visit. But then she started slipping in these other kinds of comments. "I really like my life how it is now. I like sleeping in and going out. You know, we could have a really amazing life, just the two of us. Travel. Do cool stuff. I'm not saying I don't want to have kids. It's just something to think about."

If she had said she wanted to start dating women, it would have been less jarring.

So as the "Sounds Like a Newborn" week moved along, I realized we weren't just testing whether I was ready to be a dad, but if Jill really wanted to be a mom. On the fourth night I woke with a jolt in the middle of the night. The alarm hadn't gone off, but it was due any minute, so I pulled a slip of paper from the bowl: "Reorganize the kitchen and bathroom cabinets." We had included that one as a challenge to our partnership—it was an activity that if we did it together would take half as long as it would if one of us did it alone. Heroically, Jill rose from bed to help.

She stumbled into the kitchen and started feverishly organizing and wiping shelves. Then she was in the bathroom, quickly tidying her area. And then she was back in bed. "Sorry, that's as much as I can do," she said. It was another hour before I joined her under the covers.

JILL: I knew it was pathetic, but I literally couldn't stay awake any longer. I had already been up most of the night doing laundry and had to be at work leading a group presentation in three hours when Brook pulled the partnership activity. I needed my sleep, was that so terrible? The way Brook looked at me when I went back to bed seemed to say, *Yeah, it's a little bit terrible.* My limitations were especially obvious because Brook was a total champ. The less sleep he got, the more energy he seemed to have. Six hours, four hours, it didn't matter, he was up and full of pep. A week of sleeplessness wasn't turning him into a disaster. Me? I was a different story.

The truth is, I love sleep and never seem to get enough. In the days leading up to the date, I grew genuinely concerned about how I'd manage with much, much less. I'd seen what sleeplessness could do to a family: My niece, Georgia, was a lovely, sweet baby . . . who never slept. My brother, Steve, and his wife, Noelle, spent hundreds of hours walking her in a stroller, bouncing her on a ball, rubbing her back. And even though I never heard them complain, it clearly changed their mood, their relationship, and pretty much every aspect of their lives. They were stoic about it but I looked at what they were going through and wondered if I could be so tough.

There was something else weighing on me aside from extreme exhaustion. I had been disappointed to learn after our date with Jack that Brook felt I'd been a condescending parent. Sweet old me? Impossible! If a friend had met me for coffee afterward, I would have bragged, *Brook and I were incredibly supportive co-parents. We really worked as a team of equals.*

But no, apparently not. Even worse, I'd been defensive when Brook pointed out how I stepped on his toes during the date. The first item on my FYI List was *being honest about what bothered us,* but when Brook finally told me something tough, I was hostile in response. How could I expect him to say this stuff when I wasn't willing to hear it? *Being honest about what's bothering us* was definitely staying on the list.

And my FYI List wasn't just to track Brook's flaws, it was also to help me identify and overcome my own issues. Even as my pushiness with Jack bothered Brook, I'd been absolutely oblivious to it. And that seemed really dangerous. So I added a second item to the list: *I can be overbearing.* I didn't want to spend the next fifty years as a domineering wife to a frustrated husband. And if I was tough to handle under normal conditions, how would anyone put up with me when I was a totally exhausted mom? It wasn't an issue I totally understood how to fix just yet, but it was something I wanted to be aware of as we went forward.

Early Wednesday morning, 2:43 A.M. to be exact, the alarm went off again. For the first couple of nights I had jolted awake at the first beep, but now things were getting real. I could no longer hear the buzzer unless it was accompanied by Brook's elbow. Some research has found that parents are slightly less happy than people without kids, and I started to think that was mainly because of all the sleep they're missing. "Okay, yeah, I'm up."

I had also started to think about why some people decide not to become parents. Let's face it, being a grown-up with no responsibilities is *awesome*, and having children is obviously a huge obligation no matter how much you love them. Men are allowed to admit they want to stay childless, but when a woman hints that she would rather be an auntie than a mommy she's considered selfish or naïve. Hell, I've done it myself: "You don't want kids? Oh, I bet you'll change your mind when you meet the right guy." There's so much subtle and overt pressure on women to have kids that certainly some of us are doing it even though we'd rather not. It's hard to stand up and say, "Staying childless is my choice!" As I thought more and more about my own possible transition to motherhood, I increasingly appreciated that not wanting children was a totally valid, rational life plan.

By Friday I was delirious with exhaustion and a fear of lost independence. I couldn't do anything about the exhaustion—we weren't allowed to nap—so I suggested we make the most of our possibly fleeting independence. "We've always said we want to check out Charleston; why don't we take a road trip down to South Carolina this weekend?" I held out hope we could remain active even as parents.

"With Mel?" Brook asked.

"Yeah! If we can't be adventurous with a melon, we'll never do anything with a human baby."

We wrote up some road trip–specific tasks and drove south early Saturday morning with Mel in the backseat of our rental car. A few hours down I-95 the three of us pulled over to take a family photo at South of the Border, the epic fireworks and junk emporium on the North Carolina/South Carolina line.

When we finally pulled into Charleston, all the hotels were full. As backpackers we almost never booked ahead—we liked to keep our options open—but now we had a child to consider. Mel slowly ripened in the stuffy backseat. After an hour of fruitless phone calls, we found a thin-walled motel on the sketchy outskirts of the city. The moldy-smelling air conditioner couldn't have been healthy for an infant. But we left Mel in the room with her imaginary babysitter and then yawned through a nice dinner in town. We were back in bed by 9 P.M. with our alarms set for one last sleepless night.

I woke some hours later and could just barely make out some dimly lit shapes across the room. I must have slept through the alarm because Brook was already up, pacing across the dingy carpet, gently bouncing Mel. At least that was what I decided I could see. The hazy image of a grown man attending to the needs of a watermelon suddenly struck me as both beautifully sweet and totally absurd. *I can't believe we actually did this.*

Mel cried out one last time at 5:30 A.M. My turn: "Drive around with the baby for twenty minutes." I lugged Mel through the darkened motel parking lot, managed to find our car, and started the engine.

As I sat waiting for the early-morning dew to clear off the windshield, I checked my e-mail. All week our friends had been asking about our progress and sharing their own infant war stories. Somewhere in New York, one of them was also awake at 5:30 A.M., dealing with an actual child. For once, a message that wasn't focused on vomit:

> You may be tired simulating a sleepless night, but what you can't practice is the utter euphoria of the whole experience. How you don't even realize you're tired because you're running on pure adrenaline. If only there were a way to simulate

the middle-of-the night snuggle up against your neck, it's pretty awesome.

It was sweet and true. We were practicing the horrors of early parenthood without living the joys of bringing home a real Mel. And yet somehow I felt attached to Mel. As we drove in circles through the early-morning darkness I found myself reflecting on what an adventure borrowing Jack and coddling Mel had been. I knew these were short-term simulations, but I really felt like I'd glimpsed just how exciting, life-changing, and terrifying raising a child might be. It didn't mean we'd have fewer adventures in life, just that we'd have different ones.

I had come to see that not wanting kids is a legitimate choice, it just wasn't my choice. Even during the toughest moments with Jack and Mel, I still hoped to be a mom one day. I remembered my own childhood, the softball practices and camping trips, and I wanted to live that again, but this time as the mom. I hadn't realized that my little comments about a life without kids were sending mixed messages to Brook. I was just being honest about how much our life—and our relationship—would change. That obvious truth genuinely scared me. But not enough to not want kids.

The sky was brightening as I pulled back into the motel parking lot. We'd survived! We could go back to sleeping like normal people! We would be devoted (though tired) parents! I felt almost euphoric and a little emotional as I parked, giving myself a moment to imagine our hypothetical family.

The reverie was interrupted by a heavy thud at my back. *What the hell was that?* I spun around and saw Mel lying on the floor. I hadn't strapped her in.

Timeline

JILL: Until we did the *Kids* dates I had no idea Brook had spent all these years picturing me as a mom. Hearing him talk about it made me feel both really special and totally overwhelmed by his expectations. His parenting daydreams were especially surprising because until now I hadn't allowed myself to have any of my own. Kids were something I assumed I wanted "in the future," but for the most part I avoided imagining any specifics. That's probably why my gynecologist's warning had been so jarring. With our next date, which we were calling "Timeline," we would explicitly define our hopes, separately mapping out the next several years of life milestones and then checking to see if we were on the same page.

One reason I had avoided thinking about my future in too much detail was that I prided myself on not being a stereotypical woman and girlfriend. I didn't want to be the annoying partner hinting at engagement rings, issuing ultimatums, or slowly replacing his video games with throw pillows. I was so determined not to be a cliché that I avoided doing anything that could be perceived as a nudge down the aisle. But that was only part of it. The darker, sadder truth was that I just didn't have much faith in a future with Brook the first time we dated.

Now, things were different. We'd worked through those trust issues and I believed we really might have a future. So for the first time I needed to define what I wanted that to look like.

It was harder than I expected. When I sat down to write out my hopes and plans, I realized that I'd already lived past all the expectations I ever made for myself. As a young girl I had a really clear picture of things like high school and what kind of babysitter I'd be (obviously a cool one who would let kids stay up past their bedtime). I guess I pictured college, but mostly because my parents expected it. As I got older, I tacked grad school onto my future, because why not? When I graduated with an MBA just shy of my thirtieth birthday, I had accomplished all the plans I'd ever made for myself. Since then I guess I'd been coasting.

On a blank sheet of paper I started sketching my timeline. I wrote out the next seven years (2015, 2016 . . .) and next to each wrote Brook's and my respective ages. I instantly felt overwhelmed. *Oh God, we're old. I'm dating a guy in his midthirties and he's age appropriate! Deep breaths. I can do this.* To quiet my gynecologist, I figured I'd start by listing when I wanted kids. I slotted in the birth of my last baby at age thirty-six and worried that the math would tell me I should already be a mom. But, phew, this timeline gave me three more childless years. I felt emotionally capable of that. Maybe that wasn't as soon as my doctor felt I should start, but it was . . . *Shit, I have our ages wrong.* When I made the three columns I somehow got confused about how old I was. After some reluctant recalculations I confirmed, then reconfirmed, that I was in fact a year older than I originally thought. I'd lost a year! My first baby would need to show up within twenty-four months. Sigh.

The rest of the timeline was a lot easier to fill out—I really wasn't left with many choices. Two kids would have to be enough, with a year or two in between. I added in some estimates of when I might like to live abroad and when my student loans would finally be paid off. Our wedding date went on last, in the only year between now and getting knocked up. That was also known as "next year." Deep breaths. Guess we'd better finish these forty dates sooner rather than later!

I stepped back and looked at my timeline. I'd never seen all these life events in one place before. Like on an old overhead projector from junior high, I'd layered professional, biological, and relationship transparencies on top of each other. Weird insights jumped out. I'd be nearly forty when my first kid was in kindergarten. I'd finally pay off my student loans around the time I'd want to buy a house. For the first time I had a concrete set of midlife dreams, but they looked really hard to pull off alone.

BROOK: On my own piece of paper, I started jotting down the next big milestones of life—becoming a husband, a dad, a home-owner. In a way it was strangely easy because I didn't feel like I had many choices. Five or ten years before, this exercise would have pro-duced a squishy lists of *maybes*. But the clock had pushed our future into a kind of two-minute drill.

Jill's doctor visit had been a big deal for me too. I remember her walking into our apartment that day with this terrible look on her face, like a friend had just been hit by a bus. "I went to the doctor today," she began, and I knew from the crack in her voice that the second half of the sentence wasn't something she wanted to say. She started again: "I went to the doctor today and he lectured me about starting a family before I get too old." She collapsed on the couch.

I gather from my female friends that "The Talk" with their lady doctor starts soon after their thirtieth birthdays (as if the milestone isn't harsh enough). For most women I know, the plan had been to find a guy to spend her life with, marry him, maybe enjoy a couple of years as a married couple, then have some kids. But somehow it all happened more slowly than they expected. Usually, some bozo like me was partly to blame.

Stupidly (if understandably), a lot of women (and men) seem to hope that ignoring biology will make it go away. An anonymous woman who got "The Talk" from her doctor wrote in horror to the *Washington Post*'s advice columnist: "My gynecologist asks me at every annual appointment if I'm going to try to get pregnant this year. This time, she took it a step further by lecturing me in the middle of my exam. 'You know, most women's fertility really starts to drop by age thirty-five.'" The columnist, Carolyn Hax, had some simple advice: Shoot the messenger. "You can change doctors. I hope you do, and say why."

One of my favorite quotes is from Upton Sinclair: "It is difficult to get a man to understand something when his salary depends upon his not understanding it." It also seems difficult to get a woman to acknowledge the biological advantages of having children by age thirty-five when her happiness depends on not acknowledging the facts. But if we're willing to admit that the research of scientists is a better guide than the hopes of procrastinating thirty-somethings, then the reality is clear: Things get harder after thirty-five.

So for me the significance of Jill at age thirty-five gave me something concrete to work back from. I knew I wanted at least two children, so if the last needed to be conceived before Jill's thirty-sixth birthday and we needed some time between kids, she would have to be pregnant with our first rug rat within thirty months. It actually didn't seem that daunting. Except for one part.

If I took myself off the piece of paper—if I imagined getting hit by a bus or a case of cold feet or Jill's epiphany that I wasn't the right guy—if I disappeared from Jill's life plan, her timeline was totally blown. She couldn't find someone else and beat the clock to thirty-five.

The weight of that reality settled on me for a minute because my situation was so different. I could still walk away. I was a thirty-four-year-old guy with all his hair and teeth, passable social skills, and a cool-sounding job. I would be crushed if Jill disappeared from my piece of paper, but everything on it, the two kids and the house and all the rest, would be just as available to me in five years. But not for Jill. I was her last chance at doing this the easy way. I could understand why the doctor's visit freaked her out.

When we put our two pieces of paper next to each other and they looked pretty similar, I could see the relief on Jill's face, and it surprised me. *Of course this is our plan*, I thought. It hadn't occurred to me that we'd never explicitly discussed this stuff before. It was a powerful moment for us. Right there in blue ink on white paper was a date for when we thought we might get married and another for when we hoped to have a kid.

Our plans were so similar that we immediately combined them onto one piece of paper. And then, in a twist that was too terribly perfect, a gust of wind swept through the bus we were riding and pulled the paper out an open window. This is not an imagined literary flourish or an exaggeration added for dramatic effect. It actually happened. Our carefully hand-scrawled life plan blew out a fucking bus window. You could have read that as a bad omen, but we laughed—at least the two of us were still in the bus and on the same page.

DATE #10
_____

Losing My Religion

BROOK: We flew out to California to spend Christmas with Jill's family, and it was kind of a big deal. In all our years dating we'd never really done holidays together. In the Silva-Braga household Christmas was a celebration of excessive presents and over-the-top desserts. Jill's family was devoutly Catholic, so their Christmas involved much more actual religion. On December 24 we made our way to Mass, where the Andres clan knew how to get the good seats in the crowded church; they weren't the types to only come twice a year. Jill had actually gone to the Catholic school next door and as we sat there in a side pew, she could still recite most of the service.

Even after we'd mapped out a future family, there was a pretty important part of having kids we had never discussed: How would we raise them in terms of religion?

My mom was raised Catholic, my dad Presbyterian. But we never went to church and I don't think there was a Bible in our house. I have a childhood memory of tagging along to Sunday school with a friend once, but mostly religion was this mysterious black hole I knew very little about. When I was a kid, when others would pray or discuss the Bible or cross themselves, I tried to fake my way through. It made me feel a bit like an outsider and gave me sympathy for Jews and Muslims and atheists who felt excluded by public displays of religion.

I'd always had a great respect for the faithful. I felt that if 80 percent of humanity believed in something, then there was probably something to it. So I went through life with a reverence for religion similar to my reverence for Einstein—I might not appreciate the details, but if so many smart people were on board I was going to give it the benefit of the doubt.

But I was still in that same old awkward position as I sat next to Jill, with her giggling at my efforts to follow the hymnal and her family hiding their smirks as I stayed seated during communion. I knew this stuff was more important to her family than mine, so to some extent I was willing to defer to her wishes for raising our kids. But only to a point. The weakest part of the religious argument seemed to be the idea that infants should be indoctrinated into beliefs they didn't yet understand. Even if I regretted my lack of religious experience, I didn't prefer forcing beliefs I didn't share on my kids. We still had a lot to talk about.

JILL: It's cute that Brook assumed my family got the good seats at Christmas Mass because we had insider knowledge. In reality we were just running super-late and had to sit in the shameful overflow chairs they set up at the front of the church. But having Brook and my family together in the place where I'd spent every Sunday growing up was surprisingly intense. Even though I have a long Catholic résumé, I've never been a devout believer. My family just expected me to participate in the church so I did, often kicking and screaming.

I came to think of myself as ethnically Catholic, the same way my Jewish friends were Jewish without going to temple or keeping kosher. I went to Mass with my family when I was home and randomly knew a lot about the Bible, but religion played no role in my daily life beyond that. So why did I care so much that Brook was beside me at Christmas Mass?

It probably had a lot to do with the two of us having just taken the big step of making a shared life plan. I couldn't tell if Brook felt the same way, but for me it was a game changer. Here we were admitting what we wanted; it involved each other and basically matched up! In all the years we dated we'd never been so open with each other about our life dreams—or perhaps we'd just been less confident about them. Now there was no denying we wanted the same things and that those things were coming up soon.

I knew I didn't want to be a practicing Catholic as an adult. But if Brook and I ended up together, did I want my kids to grow up completely secular? In my experience, kids who weren't exposed to religion rarely explored a faith later in life. Letting kids decide what religion they wanted to follow meant that parents were still making that choice for them; they probably wouldn't be religious at all. I made an informed decision not to be religious as an adult only after years of being exposed to the good and bad parts of faith. My parents truly gave me a choice and, though I distanced myself from Catholicism, they have always been supportive.

While participating in the church hadn't been spiritually fulfilling for me, it did provide a strong community of support and quite frankly kept me out of trouble while I was growing up. And for an hour every week my family spent quality time together. No phones, no TV, no newspaper. Just us sitting quietly next to each other. So I was stuck: I wanted that for my kids but had no interest in being a practicing Catholic.

Back in D.C. we walked up Fourteenth Street, past the church where Lyndon Johnson prayed when he was in office, and sat for dinner at our favorite Sichuan restaurant. "So, we're not religious," I said to Brook.

"I think that's right," he replied. "So it would be asking a lot to tell our kids to be religious."

"Yes, and . . ." I said. "Yes, and even though I'm not religious, my Catholic background is important to me."

This date was the first time I'd thought about how my religious background might impact my children and my spouse. Upon reflection I was surprised to find that I wanted my kids to at least receive the early sacraments—baptism, reconciliation, and first communion. I didn't want to go to church every Sunday, but I could see myself dropping the kids off at catechism class and squeezing into a pew at the holidays.

I understood Brook's hesitancy to choose a spiritual path for a child too young to understand, but I felt we could still encourage our kids to choose their own faith while teaching them my family's traditions. Brook seemed reluctantly supportive as he silently munched some spicy green beans. By the end of the meal we'd reached a decision: Our kids would receive the Catholic sacraments, barring a major religious awakening from either of us. The rest of the details were just too hazy to work out for now. Walking back to our apartment, my head spun. In the few weeks we'd been doing these *Kids* dates I felt like our relationship had changed in a significant way. My gynecologist forced me to confront the truth: I was an aging single woman who wanted a family. Ignoring biology was a dangerous game, but so was rushing into marriage and parenthood just to quiet my clock. Before Jack arrived I hadn't known for sure that Brook even wanted kids. But I'd seen not just his interest in a family but his willingness to sacrifice for one, to jump up at the sound of the alarm, to baptize his child in my family's faith, to bend his life plan to my body's timetable.

I put my arm through Brook's and squeezed his hand. I allowed myself to imagine what we'd be like as parents, walking back home from dinner behind a thick-wheeled stroller. First, though, we had to finish ironing out our viability as a couple. And the next test would force us to confront our biggest hurdle through all these years of dating.

Sex

DATE #11

Sex Notes

BROOK: The plan was simple and it sounded kind of fun. For seven days, starting at the stroke of midnight on January 1, we'd each give the other our best sexual efforts. Then at the end of the week, we'd openly discuss what had gone well and what hadn't. It seemed like a very grown-up way to nurture our sexual relationship. But since when did sex involve a scheme that sounded like a business improvement seminar?

Sex wasn't supposed to be work. It was supposed to be *magic*—the illicit spark of backseats and dorm rooms. Sex: the ultimate sign someone likes you. And if they really like you, they promise not to have sex with anyone else.

When you first start dating someone, the fact you have sex is the main thing that distinguishes the relationship from your other relationships. But then all these other things crowd in—sharing your problems, sharing your bills, sharing your DVR—until sex doesn't even seem especially important to why you're together. It's a totally evil trick: to have something pushed so far from the center of your relationship and at the same time given a singular power to end it.

For almost every couple, sex starts easy and turns difficult. For Jill and me, sex was never easy.

There's a great *Seinfeld* episode where Jerry can't kiss the girl he likes because they're "too compatible." Their conversations were so good, "there were no awkward pauses" for him to make his move. It felt like that with Jill. We had this chummy dynamic that made sex seem incongruous. And when it finally happened I felt all this added pressure because I already really liked her; *what if it's not good?*

And then it was truly, almost comically bad. Like if you went on a first date and had such an awkward hookup, you just wouldn't call them back and they wouldn't call you—but we were already best friends. We weren't going to stop hanging out, I didn't want to "just be friends." But the first awkward hookup put pressure on the next. And two awkward hookups were a pattern, and down we spun from there.

Around that time, I remember Jill mentioning a chat she had with a married friend who said not to worry if the sex wasn't good because it never stays good anyway. "Sex in a long-term relationship," she said, "is like visiting the tourist attractions of your own city." That was probably true, but when it didn't even start well, the inevitable slide took you to an especially dark place.

Could we be happy with a bad sex life? We wouldn't be the first to try. Our grandparents' generation insisted that sex should wait for marriage—no vetting in the bedroom—which meant plenty of physically incompatible people ended up together. They celebrated the self-denial of waiting until marriage as serving a greater good, which seems silly to most of us now. But I wonder sometimes if we'll seem just as silly to our grandchildren, who might manage to separate marriage and monogamy. If sex ultimately isn't central to a partnership, if it's hard to stay excited about the same person for a long time, then why have we built a system that sets us up to fail—an agreement that leads to so much temptation and pain?

"People agree to it because they think it's not a choice, and those people become serial cheaters," Jessica said. Jessica is a college friend who had just gotten engaged and was recounting how she had offered her fiancé the right to sleep with another woman once per year for as long as they were married. Maybe begrudgingly, he had returned the offer.

"People don't realize there's another choice because they think that their preference is a deficiency of character," she said. Jessica didn't want to deprive herself the excitement of hooking up with new guys just because she was making a life with one guy.

Maybe it's possible to share your life with a partner but get your sexual satisfaction elsewhere. But I've always been suspicious of schemes that ignore the realities of society. Best I could tell, nonmonogamous marriages rarely work. The emotional strain of your better half boinking someone else is probably a bit too intense for most folk.

But I also thought there was another reason nonmonogamy fails: The desire to be with other people isn't just a reality of biology; in my experience it's also a sign that your union isn't in great shape. When Jill's and my relationship was a wreck, temptation circled constantly. Now I noticed it much, much less—other women were still attractive but rarely tempting. I was pretty sure that wasn't just a sign of personal growth but also of our relationship's new strength.

When Jill and I got back together, we finally enjoyed those magic nights you're supposed to have when you first meet—we just had them four years later. And like Jill's married friend said, it never stays like that forever, but it leveled off in a much sexier place than it ever had before. But still, it leveled off. Even during this week of special effort we didn't get the job fully done. Of the seven nights we were supposed to be doing it, we managed just four.

JILL: After a week of quietly judging our sexual performance, Brook and I sat down to debrief over a bottle of wine. I assumed we'd need it.

Brook is dead on about our sexual history. Close your eyes and picture us lying in bed starting to hook up. The sheets are moving, things are happening. Now someone rises to get on top, just as the other one starts to . . . *No, go ahead . . . You . . . Sorry . . . Ouch! . . . Is your eye okay?*

For a long time I felt responsible for the awkwardness. Brook was known as this ladies' man, so he obviously knew what he was doing, right? I figured if the sex wasn't good, well, it was my fault (never mind that I'd never had this problem with anyone else). And that mind-set made me stiff, passive, and overly sensitive to any feedback Brook shared. Not so sexy. But in all those years together it was something we discussed out loud only two or three times. Mostly, we suffered silently, pretending nothing was wrong, wishing impossibly that maybe the other one didn't notice.

Brook's also right that things had changed dramatically the second time around. Maybe the biggest difference in our whole relationship was that the sex was better. When we reunited and hooked up for the first time, I woke the next morning with a rash covering half my face. "Oh no, Prom Night Makeout Massacre," Brook joked. That old awkwardness was gone. Where before his hand would indecisively brush my body, now he held me with purpose. And I grabbed back.

I couldn't inspect Brook's brain to see what had changed, but I could feel it. I had changed too. I'd shed a lot of emotional baggage after we broke up by dating some fun guys and having good sex with them. Society may look down on sex as a way for women to move on after a breakup, but for me the hooking up and flirting that year we were apart was a real positive.

But as our newfound passion wore off, I wondered what we'd do if our old problems resurfaced. Could we dig out of a rut like that? Or would we end up back in the awkward pattern of not knowing what either of us wanted and not having the confidence to ask?

So "Sex Notes" was an important test of our ability to sustain that change. If we were going to spend the rest of our lives together, we needed to make sure little tensions didn't turn into libido-killing "issues," that decades of monogamous sex wouldn't become decades of monotonous sex. We needed to practice saying some things out loud.

We both started safe in our debrief, emphasizing how great hooking up with each other was and what good partners we were . . . blah, blah, blah. We were feeding each other "compliment sandwiches"—starting with the good, mentioning the bad, then bringing it back to the good.

Niceties out of the way, I shared something I believed had a really negative impact on our sex life: the time of day we most often did it. It might seem natural to have sex at night when you're already in the bedroom, but I was least interested then. I usually hit the hay before Brook and by the time he crawled into bed I was at least half asleep and definitely not feeling super-sexy. As a result, Brook had to do more of the initiating, and that made me feel like a crappy, lazy partner. I had been hesitant to bring this up because it just sounds so cliché to say, "I'm too tired for sex," but damn it, sometimes I was too tired for sex!

So I tried to spin it into a positive: What about sex earlier in the day? "Listen, I don't want to stop having sex at the end of the night, it's just that you're not getting me at my best."

"Okay, sex earlier in the day, we can do that." He was so agreeable that I wondered why I'd waited for "Sex Notes" to bring this up.

Then it was Brook's turn to share. He was quiet for a long time, the way he tended to get when he was considering how best to phrase something. It made me nervous. "So thinking about when I've had the best sex with you, I think one common thing is that it's pretty clear in any given moment who is in control. Sometimes, when things aren't as good, it's this in-the-middle thing, where no one takes or surrenders control."

I knew exactly what he meant. "The most awkward times we've had sex, I haven't been able to tell whether you're trying to get me to do something or trying to get me to stop doing something," I said. "I can tell you're getting frustrated, but it makes me skittish, like 'What the hell do you want me to do here?'"

"Yeah," he said. "I don't know how we put that into practice, but maybe it's something to keep in mind—to decisively take charge or let the other person take charge."

We sat there quietly for a few moments sipping our wine. "Maybe when I'm feeling out of sync I slow down and kiss you more," I thought aloud. "But when you feel out of sync you're like, let's amp up the heat. Maybe that's why we feel this tension sometimes."

He nodded. Clearly we didn't have all the answers, but we were finally speaking openly. And none of the complaints were terrible, jarring truth bombs. Sex for us really was better than it had been before.

But did we have the tools, and the natural compatibility, to excite each other over the long term? When I considered our history I found myself still feeling uneasy about that. Later that night I took out my FYI List and wrote a third entry: *Are we sexually compatible?*

DATE #12

Not That Again

JILL: A business trip soon called me out of town for a day of meetings in Philadelphia. I shared a train ride home that night—and some Amtrak wine—with two other women, also thirty-somethings living with their boyfriends. We bonded at first over our similar jobs, but when the chitchat moved from office politics to men, I tried to tease out how they dealt with sex in their long-term relationships. Super-professional, I know, but they didn't need much prodding!

Brook and I were about to start "Not That Again," a date demanding a week of different sex every day, no repeats, and I wanted to hear how women in similar relationships were dealing with intimacy and compatibility.

"You know, honestly, I don't even remember the last time my boyfriend and I had sex," one of the women laughed. When she saw my face she unconvincingly added, "We've both been really busy . . ."

To fill the silence, the other woman jumped in with a story, though I doubt it made the first girl feel any better. "My sister and her husband of six years have sex every day. Every. Single. Day. It's important to her husband, so my sister just makes a point of prioritizing it. They were visiting last week and had sex in my shower before we went to dinner."

We sat there on the train for a minute, all pondering those two extremes. Better too much than too little, I guess, though 365 days of copulation sounded like a bit much, especially for two people with jobs and kids. And I wondered if having sex every day would truly foster monogamous sexual happiness. I thought about my friend Christy, who lived with her boyfriend and often complained that their life was one giant rut.

"We come home from work, order takeout, smoke weed, and watch TV. Then we fuck and fall asleep." I didn't know if high-frequency sexual ruts were as dangerous as sexless ones, but they both seemed pretty unpleasant, like choosing between an empty glass of water and a fire hose.

Night one of our Carnal Cruise buffet kicked off as soon as I got home from the train station. Brook and I hadn't written a rulebook for the date—what exactly counted as "different" sex. But it clearly couldn't be just a different position or new piece of lingerie. Which is to say we would want to save "normal sex" for when we had run out of more novel ideas.

I found Brook on the couch and we immediately enjoyed a pre-dinner hookup. It wasn't the wildest thing out there—I didn't even take my pants off—but at the end when Brook whispered, "Welcome home, babe," and kissed my sweaty forehead it felt like bliss. If we hadn't been doing the date I'm sure we would have busied ourselves with some kind of nonsense when I got home and then, best case, hooked up at the end of the night when I was half asleep. *This* was a much better scenario.

As the week unfolded we explored the architectural and anatomical options at our disposal. A Saturday morning blowjob in bed, sex in the bathroom at a friend's house party (Sorry, Ryan!). The variety was exciting and I felt really in sync with Brook. Of all the dates we'd done so far, this one seemed the most natural and most fun.

And then, as we were getting ready for bed Wednesday night . . . "I've got a truth bomb for you," Brook said. I froze and my stomach rumbled. I knew whatever secret he was about to share would be awful. God, I hated that my reaction felt like the old, timid Jill who I thought was gone. Brook continued, "I'm feeling a little like you right now. I want to have sex, but it's late and I'm tired." My whole body relaxed and I laughed. "I'm exhausted too, but we should make it happen." A few minutes later we crossed off another sex act and fell asleep entwined in our sheets and each other. I was happy. Like really happy, and it wasn't just the sex endorphins. He had told me what he was thinking, he had listened to what I said about late-night hookups, and for a night at least we felt the same way!

BROOK: Even on the seventh day, we couldn't rest. (Will I go to hell for writing that or just to Bad Joke Purgatory?). Unsure how to finish the week, we came up with something we should have done much sooner: We each scribbled three novel sexual ideas on scraps of paper and put them in a hat.

Before this date we had definitely never had sex seven days in a row; I doubt we'd even managed four. But when you're forced to choose sex over watching a movie or getting a drink, you're reminded that hooking up is pretty fun, that it brings you closer as a couple, and that doing it more is probably a good move. There's a reason people sign up for thirty-day workout challenges or download apps to help control what they eat. The truth is that even things we know are good for us can be hard to keep doing. Life's gravity keeps pulling us toward bullshit: work and television and checking our e-mail.

But our week of sexual gymnastics would only be meaningful if it prodded us to have more frequent and more creative sex for years to come, not because a silly date said we had to but because our love for each other insisted on it. All signs pointed to that being a real challenge.

You might remember Alan Simpson as that old U.S. senator who wrote a big report about reducing the national debt. But in 2014 he gave a curious interview to NPR about sex. It was a joint interview with his wife, Ann, and they wanted young couples to know what they'd learned from nearly sixty years of marriage.

"The hardest thing for all couples to talk about is sex," Ann said. "The big issues in all marriages, that hang it up, is your sexual relationship."

What made Ann and Alan Simpson's comments so striking—the reason they made headlines—was how rarely this stuff was discussed in public. "Then when you talk about that, you think, well there's a couple of horny people," the senator said. "No, that's not the point. It's called intimacy." As if to help make his point, the *Huffington Post* wrote up the juiciest bits of the interview under the headline, "Alan Simpson Doles Out the Sex Advice You Didn't Want."

It makes absolutely no sense: The thing that distinguishes a romantic relationship from other relationships, the thing that breaks up so many marriages, remains a dark, fuzzy blob of ill-defined expectations. Our best clues are also the cruelest: romantic comedies and porn, a few carefully chosen stories from our friends. What does a good sexual relationship even look like for a married couple? Any guidance—from popular culture or our closest pals—is biased by the desire to impress, to entertain, to seem normal.

One night while Jill and I were broken up, a married friend cornered me after a couple of drinks. "Have you noticed you don't last as long as you used to?" he asked.

"No," I said with the prideful honesty of a bachelor basking in sexual variety. "Maybe you just aren't as attracted to her as you used to be," I said with a shrug.

"It's not *that*," he insisted, and walked away.

Whether it was *that* or not, I'm fairly certain of something else: It was probably something he hadn't talked to his wife about. It was something I wouldn't want to talk to *my* wife about. And that's the real problem, even more than the lack of openness we have as a society about this stuff. It's the lack of openness we have as couples.

In the bedroom, under the soft glow of battery-powered candles (don't knock them; you can fall asleep and not burn down your house), we pulled one of the scraps of paper out of the hat. It directed us to be especially vocal, and we loudly finished our week of bedroom fun. Using the rules of these dates, we had been pushed into having hard, important conversations and lots of sex. Could we maintain that level of communication and intimacy? That would be the real test.

DATE #13

Can't Touch This

BROOK: Then there was one week when we had a good excuse not to be intimate, and it was weird. Weirder than I expected. And I expected it to be pretty weird. I had gently pushed for "Can't Touch This" when we made the list of dates. I wanted to see what would happen if we couldn't touch for a week. I wondered if all the hand holding and shoulder rubs were somehow draining our sexual chemistry. We were constantly touching in this vaguely chummy kind of way. Would not touching create some magic?

Our apartment was immediately transformed into a strange little obstacle course of avoided contact—My hand on her shoulder? Her legs propped on mine?—No, no, no, can't do that. When Jill came home from work, since I couldn't kiss her, we just swayed in front of each other, the inch or two between our smiling faces charged with the electricity of the end of a second date. It really did change the way we related to each other, all these little moments where I felt something artificial separating us. It reminded me of those few times we hung out while we were broken up, having to fight habit to stay apart.

There were a few physical slipups—like brushing thumbs when we exchanged a pen—but the revealing moments were the mental mistakes. "I'm really hoping we can clear out the storage locker this week," Jill said on day three, and as she made the request she grabbed my knee, the firmest touch we had all week. It seemed to me she slipped up because the knee grab was a subconscious way to soften her request. *I'm not annoyed that you haven't cleaned out the locker yet; I love and care for you*, her hand tried to say.

"You just touched me," I said, happy to have an excuse to change the subject.

"Oh my God, I did, I didn't even notice!"

So maybe it was a coincidence, or maybe it wasn't, that during this week of no contact we had our most intense relationship discussion since the night we broke up. On day four we were getting dinner at 10 P.M., and that was enough to throw our whole union into turmoil.

"I can't eat this late," Jill said as we waited for our food.

"Okay," I said. "But right now I need to work late on this project. If you're hungry earlier, why don't you just eat by yourself?"

"Because you said you wanted to eat with me."

"I do, but if our schedules don't match then just make your own plans."

It didn't seem like the kind of argument that could end a relationship. But through the whole fight—even before tears started dripping onto Jill's untouched plate—I felt the need to reach out and hold her arm, calm things down. It was like swimming in a lap pool and waiting to hit the wall so you could go in the other direction, only the wall never came and we just kept swimming and swimming toward anger. We had conceived of this as a *Sex* date, but not touching was about a lot more than not having sex.

And the fight at the restaurant was about a lot more than having dinner at 10 P.M. It was really about one of the central tensions of our relationship. Jill wanted to spend more time together than I did. She subtly inserted herself into my plans over and over again, and while I rarely minded her doing that (she was my favorite person to hang out with!), after a couple hundred straight nights of it, I boiled over. Every year or so we had this fight. But this time we couldn't finish it. We left the restaurant after our unhappy dinner but knew we couldn't go home yet, so we walked over to Thomas Circle and sat on the steps below the statue of the general on his horse.

"What the fuck are we *doing?*" Jill sobbed. "We've already *had* this conversation."

What are we *doing?* You had to be there on the steps below the horse to understand how she said that word. *Why are we still trying to fix the same broken shit?* the word said. *Why are we even together?* it asked.

Normally it wouldn't have gone that far, but then it went further.

"To be honest, spending all that time together is exhausting," I said. "It isn't a fifty-fifty thing when we're together; you're a dominant personality who does most of the talking, and that takes a toll after a while."

So there it was. After seven years of hanging out I realized what bothered me and . . . wait for it . . . actually said it to her. We sat there for a long time, waiting for a resolution that wasn't coming, watching the cars lurch around the circle through a thicket of stoplights. I had the overwhelming sense that resolution would have to wait for the end of the week.

JILL: The granite started numbing my legs as we sat there. I didn't care. I was fighting back tears trying to talk, realizing I didn't have much to say for once. I wasn't upset that Brook wanted to spend less time with me; honestly I craved some time alone at home myself. I got it. But the fact that this dynamic . . . no wait, I'll say it . . . this *ongoing problem* had been branded as *my issue* was just total bullshit. My tears were equal parts sadness and anger: sadness that we were fighting and *I-give-up-go-fuck-yourself* anger.

I had listened to Brook ask for more space over the years and had changed my behavior accordingly. I tried not to tag along to his activities and tiptoed around the apartment when he was working. Was it really my fault that he didn't proactively make plans with other people so a lot of nights he was home with me?

The fight didn't come out of the blue. I sensed all week that Brook was stewing, but rather than sharing his feelings—*Jill, I'm really stressed with work right now and I need to be focused around the clock on this*—he'd been short and frustrated with me. When the fight finally broke out during our absurdly late dinner, I felt defensive and scared. I'd spent the last few months focused on how things were different with us, how I trusted him, how much better we communicated, how much stronger our sexual chemistry was. But here was a big slap in the face suggesting that things might not actually be so different, that the same big issues were still there. Just like old times, the guy I loved was telling me I was a pathetic tagalong who cramped his style—at least that's what I heard. I was hurt that he was irritated with me, disappointed that he'd been incapable of communicating what he needed sooner, and terrified that this was the tip of a relationship iceberg. What other resentments was he secretly harboring? If this had been any other week, our moment under that statue would have ended much sooner, with fewer words and tears. Brook would have caught my eye. I would have held his gaze for several seconds with a sad half smile. A hug and a tear-flavored kiss would have followed.

But we couldn't do that now. We could only talk, and that took us to a new place. When Brook explained that my energy was overwhelming and he needed quiet time where I didn't demand his focus, I actually heard him for once. I'd been misunderstanding that feedback all these years. His old "You want to hang out with me more than I do with you" complaint wasn't quite fair or accurate, but by explaining, "It isn't a fifty-fifty thing when we're together," Brook finally got through to me. I knew I could be a handful. I literally scored 99/100 on an extroversion test I had taken a few years back. But I hadn't appreciated that my insatiable need to interact wasn't just a silly nuisance but took a significant emotional toll on Brook.

Our fight was soon "over," but it didn't feel done. There's a reason people "kiss and make up," and children are encouraged to "go hug your brother" after an argument. We even end contentious business negotiations with a handshake. Physical touch is how we signal that we're on good terms again. That night Brook and I only had our words, which quite frankly weren't enough. We slowly walked home and lay down as far apart as our queen-size mattress would allow.

I didn't sleep. I had trouble understanding how the night fit into the story of our last six years or next fifty. The best tool I had was my list, so I lay there and thought about it. On the one hand, Brook had told me what was bothering him and that felt like a *huge* step forward—our lack of communication had been the first concern I put on the FYI List. But his honesty had only underscored the second entry: *I can be overbearing.* If I had heard Brook right, it wasn't really that I was a nag or bossy, it was more that my outgoing personality overpowered and exhausted him. And those were aspects of me I worried I couldn't change. My eyes were still terribly swollen when they finally closed for the night.

Four mornings later, as the sun peeked through the window, Brook grabbed me and I shot awake. The week was over and for once Brook didn't want to sleep in; he pulled himself onto my side of the bed. It was electric to finally touch—I let him have his way until I insisted on having mine. The fight finally felt behind us.

DATE #14

Sex Seen

JILL: Thank goodness our last *Sex* date was a fun one. For two weeks, every time we saw a love scene on TV or in the movies we would re-create it ourselves. It was a welcome change of pace after our heavy week of "Can't Touch This."

On night one some friends invited us to a screening of *Dallas Buyers Club* and about a minute into the film a dying-with-AIDS Matthew McConaughey started having unprotected sex with two women at a rodeo. In the darkened theater I broke into a cold sweat. It was literally the least sexy scene of all time. And it got worse. Now bleeding, but still unaware of his HIV status, McConaughey was invited into a foursome with two prostitutes. I started to feel sick.

We had designed this date with fun and adventure in mind. I didn't think I'd be reenacting the self-destructive sex life of a dying man! We left the theater that night and never discussed, let alone reenacted, those scenes. We basically pretended we never saw the movie. Some might see that denial as failing the date, but I considered it a triumph of better judgment.

I was anxious to get back on the horse without re-creating the rodeo, but several days went by without any inspiration. I guess we just didn't watch much TV. Luckily, on Thursday night, our friend Ashley came by and asked us to put on *Scandal*. Before we could say "overacting," Kerri Washington and the president were rolling around in front of a fireplace. We didn't have a fireplace but we did have a floor, and when Ashley left we thoroughly explored it. Even Matthew McConaughey redeemed himself: We were watching *True Detective* when he had a rough kitchen tryst with Michelle Monaghan. Before that night I don't think we had made full use of our countertops.

As we neared the end of "Sex Seen," I stepped back and tried to put our last month of sexual exploration in the context of our past and possible future. Throughout the *Sex* dates we'd earned high marks in bed, I thought. I mean, we were obviously open to new things and had talked honestly about what we each wanted. In the last month there had been plenty of times we made love and plenty of times we fucked.

But in a way the *Sex* dates were as much a crutch as a hurdle; they nudged us toward doing things we normally wouldn't do. The real test of our sexual compatibility would come when we weren't focused exclusively on our sexual compatibility. Would we continue to use what we'd learned on these dates when we were no longer "required" to? I felt bullish, but I wasn't ready to cross this off my FYI List just yet. I wanted to see if we'd maintain this connection when we stressed our relationship in other ways.

But we had a little more time to practice! There was one more night of "Sex Seen," and I leadingly mentioned to Brook that Netflix was streaming *Blue Is the Warmest Color*, a French film about a girl exploring her attraction to a blue-haired stranger.

BROOK: Sweet, beautiful, precious, wonderful Jill! You crack me up. First, you stumble into a horny cowboy movie and dismiss the date (hooker-filled foursomes might be out of bounds, but what about that scene in the bathroom?) and then you stack the deck by playing a French lesbian movie! Really, you think there might be some scenes you'd like to re-create in a French lesbian movie?

But I suppose that was the fun of the date: Everything we watched became charged with the possibility of sending us on some surprising sexual escapade. When you run out of new ideas and fresh motivation, having good sex with your partner gets harder. Instead of being physical, you give in to inertia and sit down to watch TV. But we had turned that on its head! By harnessing the creative power of Hollywood's top purveyors of MPAA-approved porn, watching TV became a way to have more sex with someone I'd already had plenty of sex with.

In my first job out of college, I spent a lot of weekends in Las Vegas helping televise boxing matches. My memory of those trips is mainly a hazy mishmash of free steak dinners and late-night blackjack. But for some reason, I've kept an almost word-for-word recollection of a little exchange I had with my coworker Thomas at the bar by the elevators in the MGM Grand one night.

I had just broken up with my college girlfriend; Thomas had just celebrated his fifth anniversary. And while not every married man stayed on his best behavior during these trips, Thomas always did. "It just seems really hard to sleep with the same person for all those years," I said. "I'm not sure I could do it."

"It's something that you do together," he said. "It becomes something that you share, because you're doing it for each other. And over time it becomes this thing that you've built together—it makes you closer because you're the only place to get this thing you both want." It was the least Las Vegas-y sentiment anyone had ever uttered in the MGM Grand. "It might take some time to get to that place, but if you do, you'll see that you can do it."

It had taken twelve years. But I finally understood Thomas. The point wasn't to wait for monogamy to be easy but to overcome the fact that it was hard. If our grandchildren really do get rid of monogamy, I'm pretty sure their marriages will be easier. And weaker.

Oh, but let's be honest, *Blue Is the Warmest Color* is an excellent film to watch with your girlfriend. We actually only got through the first half of the movie that night; we paused it after an hour to catch up with the plot and leave some for later.

In-Laws, Etc.

~

In-Law Handbook

JILL: On a cold winter weekend, we flew up to Rhode Island to help Brook's sister move into her new house. Quinn and her boyfriend, Mike, had lived together for years, but only recently had become homeowners and we wanted to be part of the big move. It was "big" as a life milestone but pretty small geographically. Quinn and Mike were only moving a block from the Silva-Braga childhood home, where they had stayed for the last few months with Brook's parents, waiting for the new house to be ready. I considered living with your spouse's parents to be in-law Mt. Everest, so it seemed like the perfect moment to ask Mike to share the details of his "In-Law Handbook." Who better to give me a one-on-one debrief of how to deal with my possible new parents?

In-laws can spoil your Christmas, question your motives, even poison your whole damn relationship. I knew one woman whose boyfriend's mom made a hobby of listing my friend's faults. The unforgivable crimes included "not dressing appropriately for the golf course" and "not making the bed every morning." The sniping got so bad my friend broke up with him over it.

Another friend's mother-in-law took possession of their spare key and, while they vacationed, let herself in and rearranged their kitchen. "This way makes more sense," she proudly explained when the couple returned home. Even my own mom had a cautionary tale. Her mother in-law, my grandmother, had expected the world to pause for her daily phone call with my dad. Very sweet, but also very annoying for my mom.

Best I could tell, I wouldn't be marrying into too much of a mess. I'd first met Brook's family before they even knew to be on their best behavior, when Brook and I were still just friends. I'd tagged along on a trip to Rhode Island for Quinn's college graduation and ended up helping the Silva-Bragas throw a big cookout for the whole extended family. Even with the stress of party planning, spending time with them felt effortless. Their energy and family dynamic reminded me of the best parts of my own family.

Over the next few years I stayed on really good terms with the Silva-Bragas, but here's the thing: I barely saw them. We lived far apart and got together only a few times a year. Even though Brook and I had been seriously dating for a long while, I'd spent only one holiday with his family, a Thanksgiving several years earlier. My time with Brook's parents had been heavy on pleasantries and light on the kind of life-stressing stuff that would come up if we got married. Four months living under the same roof? That was a more realistic test. Since I didn't have that much vacation time to conduct my own research, I was counting on Mike to let me know how it went.

After a morning of painting, Mike and I ditched the new-house commotion and took a stroll together, walking through the cute little New England neighborhood where both our partners grew up. After a couple of blocks we reached a cold, rocky beach and walked along the water. Mike and I had met a bunch of times over the years but had never been alone together. While I'm loud and outgoing, Mike is quite reserved. I wasn't sure how to start the conversation, so I just dove in: What was the family really like? What tensions had they been unable to hide when he was living with them? I was hoping Mike could reveal a hint of the drama I'd have to deal with if Brook and I joined our lives.

"In my opinion, they're two of the nicest, down-to-earth people out there," Mike started. We both agreed on that and talked a bit more about their generosity. "They really want grandkids," Mike conceded. "And they wish you guys lived closer but I think they understand that you won't."

That was all interesting enough but I wanted something, well, juicier. I pressed Mike for some dirt and he finally just laughed and said, "You know, you probably know them better than I do!" I wasn't sure if Mike's deflection was genuine (maybe I did talk more in one weekend in Rhode Island than he did all year!) or if he was smartly aware that whatever he said might be read in this book by his potential in-laws.

I could relate. As I sat down to write about this date I tried and tried to describe my own concerns about Brook's family, the things I worried might one day be a problem. But I couldn't bring myself to type them. I actually felt more comfortable writing about blowjobs and infidelity than meddling in-laws. That's how tricky this in-law stuff can be.

What other bond in life is so delicate? At best, it's a relationship soufflé in permanent danger of collapse; honesty is a dubious policy. I have a friend whose older sister got engaged to a man the family was less than thrilled about. The mother told her daughter why she didn't like the fiancé, and then the daughter told her fiancé. Even though the marriage went forward, that in-law relationship was dead before the wedding cake was ordered. Never mind that the mother-in-law's concerns were ultimately correct and her son-in-law proved to be a selfish husband with an anger problem. Her daughter stuck with him and two decades later the husband and in-laws still don't speak.

It's just as complicated for the couple. One now-divorced friend coached me, "Your spouse can hate his parents, but it's never your place to talk negatively about them. Sympathize, don't criticize." Even Brook had warned me about crossing that line, reminding me after I made an overly honest comment, "You know, I can talk about my family, but that's not really your place." Message received.

Mike and I reached the end of the path and turned back toward the house where he and Quinn would be living. It was filled with the people who one day might be in-laws to both of us. So far, Mike hadn't shared anything I didn't already know, and I was disappointed that this date wasn't paying off as I hoped.

He finally broke the silence. "I couldn't think of a better family to marry into." That hit me in a strange way. I'd approached the date thinking I should uncover all the scary truths about the Silva-Bragas, but maybe this exercise was just as valuable if it confirmed what I sensed already: They're a lovely group and I easily fit in with them.

We walked into the house and Brook was up on a ladder with a roller, his dad was taping trim to prepare the next wall for painting, and his mom was already laying out the room. "Quinn, don't you think the entry table would look nice over here? It's just going to be in the way where you had it. Take a look, let's just try it here for now."

Mike caught my eye. "Yeah," he whispered. "She does do that sometimes."

BROOK: We were starting our third drink and I hoped that would help. Jill and her brother, Steve, had gone off on their own, leaving me and Steve's wife, Noelle, to analyze the Andres family. They all lived on the other side of the country, in California, but over the last six years we'd spent a decent amount of time together. They were fun, smart, good people. I didn't need Noelle to tell me that. But like Jill's trips to Rhode Island, my visits out west were always short enough for everyone to keep up appearances. I had never seen the Andres clan in a fight or even a messy house. If anything, they gave off the too-perfect impression of a Romney family Christmas card. But I knew they were real live people with human shortcomings they had so far managed to keep hidden.

Noelle started dating Steve in high school and still lived near the family, so she knew where the bodies were buried. But she wasn't eager to snitch. She didn't want to start a fight with her in-laws in the pages of some dumb book.

"I have no complaints," Noelle began. As we wrote the story of these forty dates, we could mask the identity of a friend or coworker, but Jill only had one brother and he only had one wife and Noelle could handle a couple of drinks without causing trouble. "They're really both just great people," she said. I sat there and nodded, hoping the beer still had to kick in. I took a drink myself, trying to set a good example, and also to work up the courage to ask the question I'd been avoiding. "So another in-law question I have, which seems potentially unfair but might be interesting is my impression . . . my experience with the Andres family that, I guess, I feel like I've been pretty well received by four of them more than the fifth one." I took another sip. "The fifth one being Steve."

No one had been happy when I broke up with Jill, but her brother seemed to nurse the darkest grudge. Steve had stayed a bit cold when we got back together, and even though Jill tried to screen me from it, I had stumbled on little pieces of information, clues that he had been really upset with me during the breakup.

"He's not going to like that I'm telling you this, but when you guys broke up he composed a really rough letter to you," Noelle said. "He forwarded it to me and said, 'I think I'm going to send it to Brook.' The tone was, 'How dare you! How could you do this?' And I didn't let him send it. I think he was very . . . no, I *know* he was very upset. You and Steve are just so different when it comes to relationships. I mean, he married his first girlfriend. When you and Jill broke up, the story we heard was that you have commitment issues even though you love her. So he's just like, this is my sister and I don't get it, if he loves her then be with her."

And that's the in-law baggage so many of us are stuck with: strong feelings paired with weak bonds, a relationship that captures some of the hardest parts of being in a family without the support of the good bits. Yeah, my mom might drive me crazy, but that's outweighed by three decades of love. The relationship with your in-laws asks you to give that same level of forgiveness and deference even if they (or you) haven't earned it. Steve and I might sit across from each other at the next fifty Thanksgivings whether we liked it or not.

In-laws also do something else: They hint at the deepest parts of your partner's background, what she might really be like over time and under stress. "Okay, this is the only thing that actively bothers me about them," Noelle finally said. We were nearing the end of our third drink; maybe it was working. "Their family dynamic is *very* nonconfrontational. I have to dig stuff out of Steve. Sometimes I can tell he's upset by his body language. But for him to firmly say something I have to yank it out of him. He doesn't want to hurt anyone's feelings, which I think he gets from his parents."

I knew what Noelle meant. The trait extended to Jill, who for all those bad years we were together never complained about anything. The Andres family would smile and joke their way through a house fire.

"Yeah, they're all usually really upbeat," I said to Noelle.

"Yes, that's how they can hide a dig. Because it's so upbeat," Noelle jumped in. "Their dad is the master of the upbeat backhanded compliment. He says it in such a nice way you can't be mad at him. Tom will say, 'You would never understand that, Noelle; you went to [the University of] Colorado, you're not a fancy college person.' He's actually said that to me. He means it as a joke, but it's kind of rude."

Steve and Noelle were visiting us in Washington, and just that afternoon we had gone to Arlington National Cemetery. It was awkward for me how jokey and boisterous Jill and Steve were in such a solemn place. "Usually you're around upbeat people and you think, 'They're fun,'" I said to Noelle. "But then you see them act the same way at a cemetery and you realize they don't know any other way to be."

Like in a Jimmy Buffett song, the lesson was hidden at the bottom of our third drink: Listen to the jokes, otherwise you might never hear what's bothering them. A drunk guy stumbled by our table and we had him take our picture. He asked how our date was going and we explained that it wasn't the kind of date he thought it was.

Drunk guy was intrigued. "So what's the most fucked-up thing you've discovered about the family?" he asked Noelle.

"They're not confrontational and they joke about things they want to be confrontational about," she said. The guy looked a bit confused, so Noelle kept going. "It's really not that bad at all, it's kind of lovely actually."

Jill and Steve burst back into the bar. "You guys done!?" "How'd it go?!"

DATE #16

In-Law Pen Pals

BROOK: Things seemed to warm up a bit with Steve after the visit to Washington. He had never been openly hostile, but then again our big takeaway about the Andres family was how they hide their feelings with a smile. So I sat down to write my own e-mail to him, no doubt more pleasant than the one he had drafted a couple of years before but never sent. Jill and I had decided that every day for two weeks, we would write to someone in the other's family, and I wanted to start with Steve. The idea was to get to know our potential in-laws better; since we lived so far apart, e-mails and texts were the most realistic way to do that. My Ms. Congeniality was already writing to my family all the time, so this was her way of nudging me toward doing it too.

I sat at my desk, opened Gmail, and clicked the compose button. A blank white box popped up. *Hey*, I wrote in the subject line. It was a start. I noticed I had a couple of unread messages and clicked over to them. One e-mail reminded me to vote on the date of our fantasy baseball draft, so I did that right away. *Hey, Steve*, I finally typed into the big empty box. I could tell the juices were about to start flowing any minute now. I went to ESPN.com and looked for something that would strike up a conversation. Could I initiate an e-mail about

Pablo Sandoval? It seemed like a stretch, especially given how often we wrote each other, which wasn't much.

I searched my Gmail archive for all the messages between Steve and me. Five years before he had forwarded me the link to a show on PBS. Six months later he sent a story on high-frequency trading. I continued through the list, looking for an e-mail I had initiated. And I couldn't find one. However cold Steve may have seemed, Gmail suggested he'd made more of an effort than I had.

After thirty minutes staring at the compose window, the best I could muster was a one-line message. *I keep forgetting to ask at the end of the week . . . Can I get added to your Friday trivia list?*

You can't talk to in-laws about work like you can with coworkers, or about old times like you can with friends. You probably don't share the same jokes or even the same interests (or if you do, you don't know you do). You have to be careful not to offend (is NSFW the same as NSFIL?). In a room of strangers, Jill can stir up endless conversation. I don't know where it comes from; she has some mysterious well of chatter from which to draw. That's one of the reasons we're a good couple, I guess; she has a tireless serve and I can keep hitting the ball back. I just don't start my own volley quite as well.

I never improved on my lame e-mail to Steve. And I only managed to write to Jill's sister, Paige, who works in aerospace, after a failed rocket launch made the news. I did not come close to e-mailing every day. Texting was a bit easier, so a couple of times each week I sent her father, Tom, a message during a big game and hoped he wasn't watching it on a DVR delay. Pen pals? Not quite.

JILL: On the very first morning of the date, I got a message from Brook's mom. We hadn't told our families we were making a special effort to keep in touch, she just happened to write. Nancy asked for pictures of Brook for a photo album she was making for his thirty-fifth birthday and we went back and forth about it for days, that one e-mail chain nearly fulfilling my "Pen Pals" obligations. This date was so easy!

Even though we lived pretty far from Brook's family and spent only a few days a year with them, I had been able to build a relationship with the Silva-Bragas through e-mail and text. Ten years before, I had spent a semester in London and spoke to my parents a grand total of two times. Now, long distance was easy—Skype, texting, picture sharing, Facebook. But that also raised expectations that in-laws wouldn't be strangers just because they weren't neighbors. And since I was close to my family, and Brook was close to his, it was important to me that we work on being close to each other's.

But at the end of the two weeks, when I tallied my e-mails and texts, I noticed a big gap—I had spent lots of time talking to Nancy and Quinn, which was effortless, but hardly any time communicating with his dad, John. That was harder, for some reason I couldn't quite explain.

In a conference room a couple of months before I had stood in front of a projector and done a whole presentation on sending e-mail to people you don't know. There were some fancy corporate reasons for it. "To build rapport with your long-distance staff you have to first manufacture casual conversations," I explained. "The weather, upcoming holidays, sports scores . . ." One man raised his hand with a skeptical smirk. "That sounds easy, but it feels so unnatural to chit-chat over e-mail or the phone, especially if you've never met." I pushed back. "Well, of course it's awkward at first, but real relationships are often built on a series of forced encounters. You can't expect to build rapport with no effort." He nodded, unconvinced. Now I felt like a hypocrite; I had checked the boxes of this date without actually doing the hard, important part.

Why was talking to Brook's mom so easy? It seemed to boil down to something very basic: Nancy and I were pretty damn similar. We were both chatterboxes who—to steal Brook's tennis metaphor—could volley back and forth until blisters, dehydration, and darkness finally forced us to stop. Then we'd get back on the court at first light. Our similarities helped us hit it off years ago, and they'd made it easy to stay in touch since. I always counted that as a positive, but maybe there was a downside.

For the first time it struck me that thirty-four years of listening to Nancy's commentary and questions might have lowered Brook's tolerance for that kind of chatter. Maybe having a hypertalkative mother and super-outgoing wife would get a little tiring. "You're a dominant personality who does most of the talking, and that takes a toll after a while," he had conceded during the "Can't Touch This" date. All of a sudden that comment felt scarier. I pictured Brook and me a few decades in the future: the weary husband who couldn't get a word in and the motormouth wife giving running analysis of every mundane moment of the day. There's a reason Freud warned men against marrying their moms. My FYI entry *I can be overbearing* loomed a little larger.

Not long after, while getting drinks with a friend, I learned that Brook and I were not alone in this dynamic. Jenny, my outgoing girlfriend, had actually developed techniques to smooth the extrovert/ introvert tension. "My husband and I had a really similar problem, actually. When he's home I want to talk and entertain, but sometimes he's working and I'm a distraction," she shared. "So we came up with this idea that when he puts on this old yarmulke I know he's working and I can't talk to him. Actually, sometimes I catch him putting it on and then just reading about sports."

She had one more piece of advice: "Make more plans with friends than he does so you can get your socializing needs met and he can have more alone time." Her ideas seemed doable and I was sure I could come up with more, but I wondered if these were really the kinds of tricks that would work for fifty years. When I got home that night, Brook was typing away at our kitchen table. I walked in, gave him a smile, and went silently to our bedroom.

I plopped down on our bed and grabbed my laptop. The "In-Law Pen Pals" date was done, but I felt like I wasn't finished. Brook and his dad had similar communication styles, so if I wanted to have a relationship with John, then I was going to have to purposefully serve up some volleys. *Hey, John,* began the e-mail. I was still writing when Brook finally came in.

DATE #17
_____

Stand-Ins

JILL: The next weekend we took a bus through the snow up to New York City, and since we never turned down an opportunity to spoil a good vacation (I mean, strengthen our relationship!), we decided to use this getaway as the setting for our next *In-Laws* date. The idea for "Stand-Ins" was to tap two brave friends to pretend to be Brook and me for an afternoon, giving us an idea of how others perceive our relationship. The rest of our friends would not only serve as the audience for this avant-garde performance but also suggest situations for *Brook* and *Jill* to act out.

The role of *Jill* would be played by Steph, my best friend since freshman year of high school. *Brook* would be portrayed by his friend

Jason, who quickly embraced the potentially career-defining (or friendship-ending) role. Jason was a loud, opinionated, thoughtful guy. "My impression of Brook will just be me . . ." Jason said, "but turned down to volume seven." Steph and Jason had not enjoyed any formal training in the performance arts and didn't even know each other, so obviously this was going to go great.

Dates like "Borrowing a Baby" or "Trading Credit Cards," had the specific objective of gaining experience as parents or understanding shared finances. This one just seemed like a silly thing to do. But I did hope their performance would give us a different perspective on our relationship, like when you step back from an Impressionist painting and the seemingly random colors form a mist-covered Notre Dame. Maybe there were things we couldn't make out about ourselves because we were too close to one another, too invested in this going well.

As I finally started to rally the group (dinner reservations were fast approaching and this was our last shot at doing the date), Brook asked, a little derisively, "Why don't we talk this through before you get it started." I tried to remain nice. "Well, I've been trying to plan how we'd do this date for the last couple of days but you didn't want to discuss it, so I think you missed your chance for that." The partially assembled group stood around a bit awkwardly.

"We will take it from here," Jason jumped in. "Steph and I will play you and work out how the date should be run."

"This is really just to see how people see us," *Jill* told the group. She and *Brook* handed out pens and paper, asking everyone to write scenarios for the couple to work through. "I don't see people writing things down; everyone grab a pen and write something down," *Jill* said. Steph's portrayal of me was eerily on-point. She not only captured my tone of frustrated insistence, she basically interrupted me as I was about to say the EXACT SAME THING. I had to keep reminding myself *Jill* was in charge now.

The whole scene looked a bit like an episode of "Whose Line Is It Anyway?" if Wayne Brady and Drew Carey were replaced by two random people trying improv for the first time. It was definitely funny to watch and I tried to relax, but I was still annoyed with Brook for not supporting me on this. He hadn't wanted to talk about the details of the date beforehand, so I felt like he should have stepped back and gone with the flow. As I stewed, Steph and Jason began choosing ideas from a growing pile of silly and stressful situations.

Up first: deciding what to do on a Saturday night. They quickly agreed to stay in, as long as *Jill* got a massage. Next: *Jill* and *Brook* had a heart-to-heart about a hypothetical big purchase.

Jill: "But I don't think you'd actually buy crocodile loafers."

Brook: "No, that's false. I actually care a lot about what the world thinks of how I look"—Jason took a short pause, gave a knowing look, and whispered to the audience—"but I would never actually say that part out loud."

Jason seemed to settle on vanity as Brook's principal foible, but Steph went in a different direction. *Jill* was bossy. She didn't like how *Brook* was cleaning the counters or what he had chosen for a snack. She wanted him to go grocery shopping more often. "I feel like that last one was directed at me," shouted Steph's husband Jay, who was watching from the back.

The crowd was laughing and even egging Steph on. "You need to boss people around more," our friend Deb shouted. I laughed a little too, but my feelings were getting hurt. My whole life I'd been told I was bossy. One of my earliest memories was getting a time-out in pre-K for giving orders to my fellow four-year-olds. My family loved telling stories about me bossing my brother around, and my friends joked that I effortlessly earned the Girl Scouts' Bossiness Badge. (Come to think of it, when Brook grumbled that I was "condescending" on our date with baby Jack, it sounded a lot like the same complaint.)

Clearly there was truth in Steph's depiction. I did tend to take the lead on things, and I could be forceful with my opinion. But over time I'd become resentful of the label. I wondered if people even realized how rude it was to call someone bossy. I bet they wouldn't have laughed so hard if I'd been portrayed as a pushover or a wallflower. Bossiness was somehow in its own category. And anyway, I felt like the label had been totally overblown and these anecdotes were more caricatures of me than accurate memories. I was feeling increasingly defensive as *Jill* continued steamrolling *Brook*.

What about *Brook*? Why wasn't he being annoying? I felt like an innocent ant frying under the glare of some punk kid's microscope as Brook ambled along right next to me somehow safe from the beam. Sure, I can be bossy, but did our friends and family only see that one trait when they thought of us together? I wanted to stand up and scream, *Are you all taking crazy pills? Brook is the difficult one, not me!* Of course, in the moment, I failed to see that reaction wouldn't do much for my case.

BROOK: After the curtain fell on Steph and Jason, most of the group gathered in the kitchen and reviewed the performance. Jill had some notes. "I was hoping there would be more scenes like what happened today, where I was trying to get this started and Brook made it seem like I was being an idiot even though I'd tried to talk to him about it a whole bunch of times."

"I'm not a good actor," Jason confessed unnecessarily. "Which I did warn you about."

The group scattered until just a couple of us were left in the kitchen. Jill was still unhappy. She only seemed bossy because I hadn't prepared for the date, she said. She seemed bossy because I didn't get shit done myself, she said. This was supposed to be a silly, kind of pointless date, but here we were in the quicksand of some real-deal stuff.

Did she have a point that I let things slide and she ended up coordinating most of the details of our life? Yes, she did. Was that because she was often impatient and would rather do everything herself than wait for me to do it? Yeah, that too. I mean, before we met I did lead a productive life without anyone else planning it for me. But I knew arguing that point wasn't going to help anything.

I grabbed her hand and found an empty room. Other people (like me) internalized their feelings when they were hurt, but not Jill. She became poisoned by them almost instantly and often turned visibly angry. In those moments, I'd learned, it was best just to let her vent. I held her hand and pulled her next to me. We didn't agree on why the date had gone the way it had, but that didn't matter much. We knew how to dig ourselves out of these episodes. "I'm sorry that I went off on you," she said. Wonderfully and reliably, Jill got out of a bad mood as fast as she got into one. Finally, we kissed. And though our fights didn't resolve like *Dawson's Creek* episodes with tidy lessons and disappearing problems, they usually ended with periods that started new paragraphs. This fight wasn't going to fester and recur in a week. It was part of the mystery of dating someone so long that you could find that unspoken recipe for reconciliation. We were learning how to work through our problems, and in a way that mattered more than how many problems we had.

One of the first times Jill and I hung out, all those years ago, she was wearing a "Little Miss Bossy" T-shirt. I think her parents got it for her. Yeah, I guess Jill was bossy, but it didn't bother me; I probably even liked it in a way. I was a stubborn, argumentative person too, and Jill's strong personality made it okay for me to be myself. I didn't have to worry about steamrolling her because she was too busy steamrolling me. Not *trying* to steamroll me, just being herself. When Jason and Steph tried to play us, they basically failed. I don't think they portrayed what Brook and Jill were like together so much as they portrayed how Steph and Jason would deal with dating Brook or Jill. They struggled with my unsettled work situation and Jill's strong feelings about organizing a cheese plate. It seemed hard for them. And I was struck by how much easier it was for us.

DATE #18

Survey Says

BROOK: The next week, we sat at our kitchen table and stared impatiently at Jill's laptop. We had just hit send and were starting to get the queasy feeling that comes when you imagine someone reading an e-mail that maybe you shouldn't have sent. In this case we hadn't sent an e-mail but an anonymous online survey asking thirty of our closest friends and family what they really thought of our relationship. There's a certain way people express themselves when they speak to you in person and another way they express themselves when reviewing a hotel on Travelocity. We wanted a dose of that "online comment section" honesty. Or we thought we did. We had already hit send.

We had designed a nine-question survey to find out what our

loved ones thought were the best and worst aspects of our relationship, how compatible we truly were, and what issues would ultimately cause the most tension in our relationship. It all built to the final question: Should we get married?

It seems that the only time people are really honest about your relationship is when it's over. And when Jill and I broke up, there were definitely some people who seemed to think the split was for the best. It surprised me that friends who always seemed to like Jill weren't sure about us as a couple. Maybe they were just telling me what they thought I wanted to hear: *It's over and that's a good thing.* Now those same people seemed supportive of us again. For whatever that was worth.

Jill and I made some dinner, finished it quickly, and went back to her laptop to refresh the survey results. We had responses! According to our closest friends and family we were "fun" and "adventurous." Actually, "adventurous" showed up in almost every response. People saw us as the globe-trotting, bar-crawling, adventure seekers we tried to be. "You're interesting as individuals and as a couple," one friend wrote. "It's very rare to have both! You don't always agree, but at least you listen to each other." This was good stuff!

But. There were a bunch of *buts.* We suffered from a "lack of communication" and sometimes "take each other for granted." Jill was "stubborn" and I was "moody." When it came time to rate our compatibility, a third of them didn't think we were "a great match."

In all, twenty-three people responded and it was, at best, a qualified endorsement. We didn't know who, but one of the people closest to us said, "They're not right for each other." That legitimately stung. Like any insult, it hurt in proportion to the amount you agreed with it. And there was a part of me that sat back and thought, *Yes, they're right, we've stumbled into this big relationship again because it feels familiar, but that's not a good enough reason to spend my whole life with a person. Look at all these things they've noticed we're bad at.*

And then I thought, *Wait a minute, who the fuck are they?* Yes, we may have explicitly asked them to "please answer these questions," but what did their opinion matter? The whole point of a relationship is that it's between two people. Everyone else were fans in a stadium: They could offer encouragement or boo or shout dumb advice from the bleachers, but we were the only two on the field.

JILL: The negative responses really took the wind out of our sails. I think we both expected the feedback to be overwhelmingly, "Get your asses down the aisle," so when we sat at our kitchen table looking at tepid results it was a real shock. I guess it was better to hear these concerns now than at the "Speak now or forever hold your peace" stage. Even though we'd asked for the critique, it was hard to hear. But the human brain is an amazing thing and just as I was getting down about the responses, I subconsciously started seeing only the positive trends I had hoped for.

"Look, Brook, ninety-one percent said we're either a great match or pretty good together!" (I didn't mention how many picked "pretty good together." Maybe I had a future as a biased pollster.) I also found it encouraging that literally every respondent described us with words like "fun," "adventurous," or "intelligent." I'd heard people describe us that way here and there, but seeing it repeated over and over made me realize how people noticed the same aspects of our relationship that I really loved.

But for all the good I found, and I dug deep for positives, the bottom line was drawn brightly on my computer screen. Sacrifice and compromise showed up time and time again as weaknesses. "Both

seem to want their own way and neither likes to be told what to do."
"Brook seems to get his way more often than Jill does." A third of our
friends and family weren't sure we should get married. Sigh. Brook
was able to brush it off pretty easily; he just stood up and moved
on with his night. I stayed seated and started wading through the
responses.

It just felt totally insane that so many of them were unsure that
we should marry. I mean, we were great together! People had to see
that. We were funny and interesting, with complementary outlooks
on life. Spending time together was easy and when we curled up
next to each other I could sometimes feel my heart swelling with
happiness. (One time I actually Googled that feeling because the
physical sensation was so strong. Weirdly, I couldn't find any medi-
cal basis for it.)

A big realization struck me in this defensive moment: how rare
thinking positively about our relationship had become. During these
dates I'd been focused on our problems, picking apart every short-
coming I could find. But I think that singular focus was actually col-
oring my opinion of our relationship. Stepping back and building a
case for why our friends and family were wrong reminded me of all
the things I loved about us.

At its best, this Marriage Test shined a light on problems we'd
overlooked or issues we avoided confronting. But at its worst, it felt
like we'd put our relationship up on a pedestal and instead of admiring its beauty we were circling its faults. The exercise had been useful
and scary, but it felt good to take a break from it and just be positive
for a moment. The love we shared and the problems we had overcome
mattered at least as much as our shortcomings.

I finally mustered the courage to review the "unsure if we should
marry" feedback. It turned out the "unsure" group fell into three camps:

people who didn't believe in marriage in general, didn't think it was their decision to make, or felt our overanalysis was concerning. I discounted the first two groups; those respondents would have checked the "unsure" box for any couple.

It was the last group who had the best point, certainly one I'd reflected on myself over the course of these dates. Did we really need so much information to make this marriage decision? Can love and compatibility really be broken down into an equation with a clear yes or no answer? I guess the best rebuttal I had that night and throughout this test was simple: Brook and I treated the vows of marriage with the utmost respect and before entering into a lifelong commitment—for good and bad, in sickness and in health—we wanted to make sure we got the decision right. Who knows if this forty-date test was the best way to get it right. But it was our way and I didn't think a willingness to test our relationship meant marriage wasn't a good idea. It was just one more unorthodox thing Brook and I were in sync about.

DATE #19

In-Law Bucket List

JILL: "When you think about Brook's future," I began, "what do you hope he's able to accomplish?" It had been a couple of weeks since we finished the survey, and now we were conducting a kind of focus group. I was sitting across from Brook's parents, John and Nancy, for our last *In-Laws* date. I was asking for their "Brook bucket list," their hopes and dreams for his future. Brook would do the same with my parents.

I hadn't given much thought to what they might say, aside from hoping they didn't have any plans for him that were incompatible with my own life dreams. But that was precisely the risk of this date, and one of the big hazards of the in-law relationship in general: *What if my spouse is pulled by his family in a direction I don't want to go?*

A high school friend of mine moved to Italy right after college to teach English. A few months later she had an Italian boyfriend. A few years later, she had an Italian husband and a permanent life in Tuscany. Her parents had expected her to return to America, so there was real tension as they slowly said *arrivederci* to their vision for her future. You could see how a partner can be blamed for crushing a parent's dream for their child, or how a parent's influence can get in the way of a couple's plans.

"Well," Nancy started, "we hope you know how much we love you, and love you and Brook together. So my first hope is that you two are able to build a life together. And that he's able to become a father because I think he's going to be a great dad." If only Brook moved as fast as his mom! But the look on her face told me this was a genuine compliment of me as well. I never really thought they didn't like me or hoped Brook would end up with someone else, but the fact that their first wish for Brook included me felt special. I was already tearing up a little picturing them as grandparents to my children. I hadn't expected this date to be so emotional!

Brook's dad continued, "The overall thing I really hope for Brook and for you is that you feel fulfilled and respected and loved as parents and spouses. And that you can make mistakes and be angry and do stupid things and know that you're still loved, because that's not necessarily easy." Brook's parents had been married for more than thirty years, so these hopes seemed to reflect the realities of what it takes to make a marriage last.

I wondered if they had any other, more practical hopes for Brook, something of the "Don't move to Italy" variety. Nancy had a thought right away: "I hope that he's able to be a journalist in a venue that people are going to watch and see. And that he allows himself to feel successful with the work he does." Again, we were on the same page. This was one of my most immediate hopes for Brook. Not because I wanted him to make more money or have a higher-profile job, but because I wanted him to achieve his professional goals and feel proud of the work he did. I may not have been around like John and Nancy to see teenage Brook create that life goal for himself, but I hoped to help him achieve it.

And then an interesting thing happened. His parents started asking me questions about Brook's life, things that his live-in girlfriend had more insight into than they did. Like what was this new job he'd been talking about? Did I think he'd consider that a successful step in his career? All of a sudden the tables were turned; I was no longer looking for their feedback, I was the expert on Brook and his life, foreshadowing the shift that comes with marriage. Our parents have known us the longest, but our spouses eventually know us best. I can see how that might cause conflict in some families, but I liked that John, Nancy, and I could all talk about Brook, piecing together his past and present in a way no other three people could.

BROOK: We sat outside at a round plastic table and Tom assumed a very businesslike expression. "What is the purpose of this meeting?" he asked mock-seriously. "This is a *date*?" I was finally face-to-face with the actual in-laws, Tom and Jan. They were what you'd expect from Jill's parents: jovial, smart, successful. They ran their own small accounting firm serving Bay Area artists and gave off the vibe of doctoral candidates who could still make friends in a freshman dorm but wouldn't be caught dead living there. They were the only couple driving a Tesla to a Scissors for Lefty concert while calculating the tax consequences of the outing.

Jan started with what seemed like a simple wish. "I would hope that if she wants to, Jill can combine a marriage with a career and a family." Jan's own experience couldn't have been far from her mind. She'd served as Tom's CPA deputy for most of her working life, making it hard to establish her own professional identity while raising three kids. "Not that raising a family isn't a great thing, but Jill can have more than that and sometimes women lose sight of who they are. I hope Jill can do it all because she has so much potential and so much enthusiasm."

"I agree with everything she said," Tom added.

"Well, you don't have to agree because we are two separate people," Jan said.

"I know, but I do fully agree."

Jan went on. "Jill doesn't truly get sad very often," she said. "I haven't seen a lot of true sadness in her life, and the unhappiest I've ever seen her was when you two broke up. I hope in the future that if Jill should experience that kind of sadness in her life, this time you will be there with her to go through that sadness together." *And not be the cause of it*, she didn't bother saying.

It was a gentle way of mentioning our breakup for the first time since it happened. Tom and Jan had been good, silent soldiers through it all. They welcomed me back into their family without any noticeable glares. But this was their chance—their invitation—to be protective parents.

"I want you to love Jill and *accept* her love," Tom said finally. "Andres are reliable people; once we say we're going to do something, we do it. And if Jill says she's going to marry you, she is marrying you and we're all marrying you for that matter and that's fine. So I expect reliability from you. And you don't have to be reliable for much. Except to love my daughter." It was just like Noelle told me in the very first *In-Laws* date; Tom said it so nicely it didn't even sound like a dad telling his potential son-in-law not to mess with his daughter again.

But like any good locker room speech, he ended with a pep talk. "I've told other people this, though I've never told you: I feel very confident in you. I know you'll make your way in whatever you do."

As we stood up and shared a hug, Jan got in a last word. "Don't lose sight of the things that made you happy in the beginning. Some of that might go on hiatus if life gets in the way, but I hope it's always a part of you. It's important to have fun."

"That's the good thing about Jan and me, we still have fun together. She just bought tickets for me to a Todd Rundgren concert and I told her, 'There's no one else I know who would want to see Todd Rundgren,' and it's pretty cool."

Jill and I are not going to be suburban accountants. We don't like Todd Rundgren. But hanging out with Tom and Jan made it easy to see how Jill became the adventurous, accomplished, loyal woman I loved. Your in-laws are like the carpenters who built your house— the quirks, or even the faults, of the guy who shingled the roof have nothing to do with the life you make within the walls he built.

The words actually caught in my throat: "Jill didn't happen by accident. And I know you two are more responsible for that than anyone. So I appreciate that."

Communication

Test Your Love

BROOK: Well, this was stupid. For the first half of our forty dates I had been an agreeable, open-minded, thoughtful partner . . . if I do say so myself. But now we were getting into some real touchy-feely nonsense. I had just returned from a weeklong project in Arkansas and was losing my appetite for some of these dates. On the first nice day of the year, a false spring Saturday, we lugged a heavy bag of books to the National Sculpture Garden for a working picnic and found a dewy patch of grass in the sun. We had provisions from a French bakery, so it started okay, but then we opened the bag of books.

They were relationship books (I mean, who reads relationship books, am I right?), and they promised to fix our relationship through the power of brief questionnaires. In a way, our whole Marriage Test was based on the belief that these books were bullshit, that one-size-fits-all love advice is cut from the same cloth as fad diets and get-rich-quick schemes. They're good for filling space on talk shows and bestseller lists, but that's about it. But then we went and bought three of these books, so I guess the joke was on us.

Our self-help library included the grand dame of togetherness tomes, the Atkins Diet of Affection, *The 5 Love Languages*. The book's main message is that each of us gives and receives love in our own way and that by understanding what is important to our partner we can make them feel more loved. I didn't mind the premise, but when we started taking the Love Languages quiz I got that uneasy feeling you may have experienced while watching an infomercial. The questionnaire was filled with awkward either/or prompts like "I feel whole when we hug," or "What you do affects me more than what you say." I don't know. Both? Neither?

The results didn't seem especially scientific or surprising, but they did spur a worthwhile conversation. We both ranked quality time toward the top of our lists, and that led us to an obvious conclusion we somehow hadn't reached before: Since being together is so important, long stretches apart are especially hard on us as a couple. We had learned to deal with brief business trips, but spending more than a few weeks apart always led to difficulties. So even if some amazing work opportunity presented itself, we decided we wouldn't allow long-term long distance. Score one for the Love Languages! And let's buy those "As Seen on TV" knives while we're at it!

Actually, these self-help books capitalize on a clever trick: If 80 percent of success in life is just showing up, then 80 percent of success in communicating is actively trying to communicate. "Communication" isn't making sound with your mouth; if it were, Jill and I could have skipped these dates and moved straight to chapter seven, which I'd been promised was "Watching Sports While Drinking Craft Beer." No, sadly, communication is the conscious effort to work through things that don't sort themselves out on their own. It is the successful transmission of a constructive thought. It sounds so simple; why is it so hard? Well, for starters, we only notice how well we're communicating when it isn't going well. "Hey, honey, remember how I asked you to pick up my parents at the airport while you were falling asleep last night and then you remembered? That was great communication," said no one ever.

But mainly communication is hard because we don't actively, thoughtfully do it. Especially guys. Guys are the worst. I spent a lot of hours in coffee shops writing this book, and every time I ended up next to two women they seemed to be sharing something deep and meaningful about their relationships. That was so weird to me. Guys just don't naturally do that. It's almost like men and women are from different planets! So when a book comes along with the 13 Step Relationship Pyramid Flowchart Method, it kind of works just by making us show up.

Skeptical of *The 5 Love Languages*, I searched for another online test and found one that was even more poorly constructed! After we filled out the "Relationship Compatibility" questionnaire, the site spit back our precise level of affinity: "Your raw similarity score is 39%, which puts you in the 1% percentile of compatibility, which means 99% of couples . . . are more similar than you."

It turned out the website was just really buggy, but whatever; the results pushed us to discuss something useful: physical fitness, a true area of incompatibility for Jill and me. I cared a lot about work-

ing out—maybe more than I should have. Jill always found something else to prioritize. (In a stunning display of subtlety, the online
quiz actually labeled this category "Obesity.")

Jill certainly wasn't obese and I wasn't Channing Tatum, but
there was a legitimate imbalance. It wasn't something we fought
about, or even talked about. It just kind of hung out there, unspoken,
whenever I went for a run or did push-ups in our apartment or heard
Jill complain that she didn't have time to work out even though she'd
really like to. Just once or twice, when her excuses sounded especially far-fetched, had I pointed out that the only period in the many
years we'd known each other when she found time to get into better
shape was the year we were broken up. Then it seemed to matter to
her, but never when we were together.

"I come home from work and I'm just like, 'I'm tired, I don't want
to work out,'" Jill said. "I've tried and it just doesn't happen. It's actually something I've tried to work on. Why can't I motivate myself to
do this thing that's good for me? I don't get it really . . . but I cannot
make it matter to me."

Of course the dumbest thing you can do is hope to change your
partner. We all know this. But if you've ever fallen in love, then
you've held someone's hand and thought, "What if she was just like
she is, except _____." That is straight-up human nature. The
_____ could be one unavoidable truth or a long list of different
stuff or something that seemed unimportant at first but hardens
with time. Every relationship came down to the _____ and the
calculation of whether you could live with what wasn't how you
hoped. But first you tried to shrink the _____ and that wasn't all
dumb. That was part of what these forty dates were about.

But on the blanket in the sculpture garden, Jill looked up from
the get-happy-quick books and made sure I was listening. There

were some things that would never matter to her no matter how much they mattered to me.

JILL: After twenty dates we'd finally hit the sorest of subjects: my weight. Whether you called it "Fitness" or "Obesity" or "Have Your Sorority Sisters Use a Magic Marker to Circle the Fat on Your Naked Body," it wasn't something I was eager to discuss. I knew improving our communication would take work, but I assumed we'd practice on a less toxic topic. I picked nervously at the wet grass around our blanket. I had told Brook the grass was too wet to sit there, but he insisted. Here we were, on a beautiful almost-spring day surrounded by America's great sculptures having a rational adult conversation about the shape of me.

At 5'8" and 168 pounds I was by no means plus-sized, just curvy and a little soft. The Internet calculated my BMI as 25.5, just barely "overweight" but far from "obese." But Brook worked out pretty regularly so I could tell that in his eyes, I was lazy for not prioritizing exercise. He was right, I did make a million excuses for not getting into a healthy routine. And unfortunately, I couldn't dismiss him for demanding I become skinny because that wasn't what he wanted.

I thought back to this insane relay race he talked me into doing a few years before, where eight of us ran two hundred miles in thirty-something hours. He'd been so supportive and proud of me, not because I was burning calories, but because he and I were being active together. He wanted me to maintain that healthy lifestyle with him in the long term.

But I was ashamed we had to talk about this. It was *such* a sensitive topic, no wonder most people steered clear. I mean, of course I wanted to exercise more. Everyone wants to exercise more. But as all those dusty treadmills-cum-clothes-heaps attest, actually doing it is much harder. And we were still young and childless—these were the easy years! If we did marry and have kids, would he think I was gross or lazy if I couldn't lose the baby weight? Would we end up having sex with the lights off because I was ashamed of my body? I'd read enough advice columns to know this was no small issue.

So just as Brook seemed to be struggling to accept me as I was, I was unsure if I could live my whole life with the pressure to always stay fit. We were suddenly debating big scary questions about lifestyle compatibility and attraction, all because we took some random broken online quiz. The FYI List fattened as I added a fourth item: *Can I handle lifelong pressure to work out?*

Now twenty dates deep, my list pointed out that (1) Brook and I had trouble being honest about what was bothering us, (2) I was overbearing, (3) we were potentially sexually incompatible, and (4) I might spend the rest of my life feeling guilty if I didn't work out. Yikes. I thought back to my naïve kayaking self, the one who thought our Marriage Test was going to be a breeze. Little did she know . . .

While I hated talking about obesity, I didn't buy into Brook's total distaste for these tests; I actually found them pretty useful. *The 5 Love Languages* ranked the ways we receive love and Brook's top category was "Acts of Service," which was interesting to begin with and got more meaningful when he started explaining just what that meant to him.

"I'm not talking about making dinner for each other," he said. "Because that's more like a chore. I mean grander sacrifices, like when I wanted to go to the Supreme Court and had to wait in line outside for two days. You knew you wouldn't be able to go in, but still camped out there in the cold to keep me company. That kind of selfless stuff strikes some deep emotional chord in me, even if I see it in a movie or commercial."

"Huh," I said, thinking about that. "So we just have a different sense of that. If I worked late and walked in the door to see dinner ready, I'd see that as an 'Act of Service,' even though you're going to eat too." It sounded like a silly little difference, but in a concrete way it helped me decipher what made Brook feel happy and loved.

Brook fiddled with the last scraps of bread and cheese. I could tell he was itchy to finish, but since he had to pretend he wasn't getting wet from the damp grass he'd made us sit on, I pulled out one last book. We determined our Myers-Briggs personality types (me: ENFP, Brook: ENTJ) and flipped to a description of common frustrations couples like us face: how we make decisions and how we communicate. True enough. Exhibit A: this soaking wet blanket. As I started to gather up the books, I noticed a section of the Myers-Briggs book we'd overlooked, "The Joys of ENTJ and ENFP."

"ENTJs [Brook] typically help ENFPs [Jill] accomplish their many good ideas by encouraging them to follow through on complicated tasks." The very fact that we were halfway through this forty-date adventure and turning it into a book was evidence of that. There's no chance I would have followed through on something so long-term and high-risk without Brook's encouragement.

Meanwhile, ENFPs [Jill] help "ENTJs [Brook] learn how to listen more patiently, express their feelings more readily, and generally become more compassionate." A-ha! Being emotionally open wasn't natural for Brook's personality type, but my personality seemed like a good match to help him overcome that. In a way, Brook voicing his frustrations about my exercising, which he knew would be an unpopular topic, was a good sign. He was expressing himself more readily; it was evidence that one of our core problems was actually improving.

Our asses were now thoroughly soaked. We packed up the picnic and started biking home, dodging tourists lined up outside the

National Archives. We were half done with our Marriage Test. It was definitely proving to be worthwhile, just nothing like I'd imagined. At the start, I figured each date would yield a black-or-white result: "Yes, we're compatible about money but not kids." Then we'd put our results on some scale and make our decision.

In reality, we were well suited and badly matched in lots of these categories. What the dates did was stir up all this new information, and put all these new questions in front of us. That had been the goal, to force us to face different kinds of challenges. But sometimes it felt like we were passing and sometimes I wasn't so sure. What curve were we supposed to grade on?

We went up Ninth Street, then turned onto K Street toward home. On the left, we rode past the Hyatt where we had gone speed dating five months before. I thought back to that night, to how I felt about Brook then and how I felt about our future. Something *was* different now. Clearer. Brook had always been somewhat of a mystery to me, but a bit less so after every date. The blank spots in the puzzle were getting filled in more quickly than they had in those previous years we spent together. Some of the pieces that locked in most tightly were disappointing—why did he have to care how much I exercised?—but at least I could see more plainly what the finished picture might look like.

DATE #21

Silent Night

JILL: A few mornings later, I snuck out of bed as Brook slept, got ready for work, and walked out the front door. It was a normal morning, except for one thing: We wouldn't have been able to speak even if he had been awake. We were spending twenty-four hours totally silent, testing our nonverbal communication chops. Or at least that was the stated plan. But part of me suspected Brook had come up with this date as a not-so-subtle test of my ability to keep quiet for that long.

This would not be easy, as several of our dates had already suggested. I was the same Jill Andres who had been voted class clown of Justin-Siena High School after more than a handful of teachers separated me from the rest of the class to stop me from distracting the other kids. One Spanish teacher actually forced me to sit backward in the corner of the classroom for a week as punishment for excessive *hablar*ing. In her defense, I was super-disruptive. In my defense, she was the worst and her class was boring.

I'd always considered my outgoing chattiness a real strength, so it was pretty demoralizing during these dates to hear not just Brook but some of my closest friends and family point out the drawbacks to my deep well of insightful musings.

My talkativeness was what made me *me*. It had helped me make friends easily at school, rake in tips after college as a chatty cocktail waitress, and then land a lucrative and interesting career presenting to large corporate audiences. One of the greatest compliments I ever received was when my friend Brie said I was like a fireplace everyone wanted to gather around. But these dates were helping me understand that when I burned too brightly there might not be enough oxygen left for everyone else.

I had grand plans for this date. I was going to tame my burning verbosity and learn to enjoy silence. I was going to practice connecting with Brook without leaning on my words. I was going to have so much material to discuss with him the next day! When I came home that evening I found Brook working away at our kitchen table. We exchanged sly smiles as I shed my shoes and dropped my bag. Not a word was spoken.

I busied myself with some light reading on the couch and just relaxed. I have to say, it was immediately obvious that removing the option to talk made it much easier to just disconnect and do my own thing while Brook was in the same room. I certainly had a lot to share with him about my day and wanted to hear about his, but as the minutes ticked by that seemed increasingly unnecessary.

I started to get hungry. Silently I got up, walked to the kitchen and made chopping, stirring, and chewing motions to Brook. He quickly was next to me with a knife in hand. My miming skills must have been rusty because I meant to communicate, "Hey, I'll make dinner while you work," but now he was getting involved in meal prep, one of our toughest collaborative efforts. We both have our own ways of doing things and don't really like to be managed, so I was legitimately worried how we'd divide tasks and get a meal on the table silently.

But weirdly, it seemed easier that night. We both just sort of started doing stuff, grunting occasionally to confirm we should chop the zucchini or put the pasta in the water. We couldn't critique each other's choices or express frustration that the water wasn't being boiled the way we preferred. Instead we just partnered up and cooked. It was refreshing and the final product not only tasted great but came without our usual side of frustration.

BROOK: We brought the dirty plates to the sink and silently washed them. The only sound was running water and clinking dishes; it was like a movie that was just playing the background noise. But for me there was a dialogue. A transmission of thoughts. They were simple, because they had to be, but they were refreshingly clear. *I'm going to do this dish. Should I turn on music? I'm lighting this candle.* We didn't get to ask, "What music do you want me to put on?"

or "Where are the better candles?" or "Did you send in the credit card payment?"

I didn't really mind that Jill talked too much. But there were times when we weren't really saying much of anything. We were filling space with sound just to remind each other we were there. *Work story. News article. Marco. Polo.* Mostly the chatter was comforting; it was the thing we'd always been good at since those first nights in those divey New York bars. We could sit together and talk. But as your life gets more complicated and there's more real stuff to deal with, those little conversations can become the place to dump frustrations and settle scores. In the early days our first thought when we sat together was about a new song or dramatic touchdown. Now it was whether we'd paid the Internet bill.

The self-help quizzes had shown that even a dubious book can help you communicate by encouraging conversations you'd otherwise avoid. This silent night allowed us to communicate by stripping away the conversational clutter. In the silence we curled up on the couch and watched a muted basketball game. I could hear the air when she exhaled and feel the back of her heart nudge my chest. By the second quarter we were having sex.

We spent most of the night physically close, finally gesturing that we would brush our teeth and go to bed. We had to look each other in the eye to say that. We had to confirm that we were understood before we moved on to something else. The next morning, Jill told me she hadn't loved the date. The silence was weirdly distracting, she said. I said I thought it was kind of nice and tried to explain why. But we didn't get to say any of that as we crawled into bed; we were reduced to simple things: the way we felt touching each other, the thoughts we had for our relationship when we weren't discussing our relationship, our hopes for the weekend. In the silence I felt . . . comfort.

It's a Chore

BROOK: Stepping out of bed that next morning—and every morning—I navigated a sea of discarded T-shirts and orphaned jeans on the way to our bathroom. I lifted up the toilet seat and did not notice the layer of unclean covering it. I brushed my teeth and glanced into a water-stained mirror. I could not see the water stains, or the spattered grease on the kitchen floor, or the stack of mail on the dining table, or the dust bunnies mating below our couch. I don't know why that stuff didn't register, I just had some special ability to believe the apartment had always looked like that. I could see the dirty dishes, though, so I went to the sink and washed them. I always washed the dishes.

Jill and I had reached a silent, displeased détente over the cleanliness of our apartment. We discussed it rarely, and never productively, so we thought if we could just learn to communicate about this concrete thing—how we clean our home—we might be better at communicating about everything else. We squared off on neutral ground, seated at opposite ends of our couch, each clutching a legal pad filled with hand-scrawled notes outlining our housework objectives. I wondered if this was how Henry Kissinger negotiated chores with his wife. They probably had a maid.

I didn't start by mentioning the dishes. That was too fraught. A week before, when Jill was discussing some chore I hadn't done (you'll notice I said "discussing" instead of "complaining about" because I'm being considerate and diplomatic), I conceded that I might not clean the toilet, in part because I didn't even really notice it was dirty, but I did wash all the damn dishes.

"You think you do more dishes than me?" she had said.

Oh Lord. Oh Lord no. Don't tell me we couldn't even agree on this. I did so many damn dishes. I didn't even mind, I kind of liked doing dishes in some weird way. It gave me a little sense of accomplishment, it took my mind off whatever else I would be thinking about, it was the closest I came to meditating. But I digress.

I wouldn't mention the dishes as we discussed our chores, I would just list off the things I thought we could improve on, starting in the living room where we were sitting. "We need to sweep and mop the floor. And we need to get rid of the clutter, like the big cardboard box by the couch. That needs to get out of here."

The box was mine. I'd left it there for over a month, which wasn't cool. But you see what I did there—I started by mentioning things that were *my* fault. It was considerate. It was diplomatic. This was probably how Kissinger did it.

I finished my living room list and gave Jill the floor. "For the last three weeks there's been stuff on the floor," she began. "It's almost like garbage dripped all over there." She pointed helpfully to our entryway. "So I walk in and feel troubled by that every day because our house is filthy, and we actually have stains all over the floor, but then I was like, 'I'm not cleaning it because we're going to talk about it . . .' So do you, like, not notice it?"

Jill got up from the couch for a site visit to the offending patch of parquet. "We never sweep and we certainly never mop our floor."

"Well, I actually sw—"

"You sweep like a little spot if you feel something stuck to your feet. I'm talking about fully cleaning the floor." Actually I did sweep the floor. I did it mainly when Jill was at work, and I mopped the floor less often, probably every few months, but that wasn't never.

"I know what a swept floor looks like," she said. *Well, fuck you,* I thought. But I didn't say anything. I just sat there, annoyed. I'd like to say it was a negotiating tactic I learned in a Henry Kissinger book, but I just didn't have anything to say at that point. Jill insisted we didn't clean the floor. I said I did. She seemed to say, *Whatever you're doing is as good as doing nothing.*

She continued. "Our bathroom is disgusting at almost all times. Since you're the boy and you lift up the seat more often than I do, if you ever notice it's dirty, one option you have—I'm sounding like such a bitch right now but I've kept this inside for two years—is just to take some toilet paper and wipe it around the toilet bowl rim, thus making it look less like there's shit all over it."

We both laughed nervously at each other because we weren't sure what else to do. It was kind of funny, and kind of not at all funny. As a solution to our dirty apartment, the summit was not turning into a diplomatic triumph. But as an examination of our communication, there was clear value in the ordeal.

A lot of it came down to expectations and respect. She wanted the floor cleaned more often then I cleaned it, so, in her eyes, my effort didn't count for anything. When it came to the kitchen counter, our roles were reversed. She proudly wiped it down every day or two, but I still felt a film of junk on it—I told her I preferred to remove all the appliances and really scrub it clean. So I didn't give her any credit for wiping the counter.

But the unmentioned dishes were the purest example of our conflict. We both felt like we did more work than the other gave us credit for. Perhaps that was human nature—exaggerating your own contribution and not always noticing the other person's. Add a companion phenomenon—thinking most of the mess was caused by the other person!—and it was a real Cold War. "I'm just trying to be honest with you," Jill said. "This is why we're doing this date, I think most of the junk in our house is your junk." *Thanks.*

But if I'm being honest with myself, I did it too: I gave myself lots of credit for washing so many dishes without acknowledging that I created most of the dishes. I was mostly cleaning up after myself by washing them. But all of this fueled a big disconnect, this feeling that the other person wasn't pulling their weight. *They* don't appreciate everything *I* do. And since we weren't very good at communicating that frustration, it sat there misunderstood, each of us silently stewing as the other disappointed us.

JILL: We walked into our bedroom where weeks of my work clothes were piled on the floor. I was not a neat freak. But like most women, I felt a responsibility to keep our home relatively clean. Not just a responsibility, a need, a desire sprung from somewhere deep inside. As Brook and I angrily surveyed our filthy apartment I couldn't help thinking, *God, my mom would be so disappointed if she saw this mess.* When I was growing up, she had spent countless hours washing dishes and organizing toys, struggling endlessly to contain a family of five's filth. It caused her constant anxiety to see the house untidy, so she kept rolling the boulder of cleanliness up the mountain of our mess. Everything was dirty again the next day.

The apple could fall only so far from the Pine-Sol tree. I felt anxious when I noticed food stains on the stove or windowsills covered in dust. But my standards were a far cry from my mom's. More like, I don't know, maybe mop once a month? Clean out the fridge if milk spills? Wipe off piss and hair from the toilet bowl if you see it? It's not like these chores were in danger of consuming our lives. But somehow they seemed to fall to me. And I knew if we had company our guests wouldn't say, "Wow, Brook really is a slob." They'd think, "Wow, Jill doesn't clean much." It was just another double standard of our post–women's lib society.

For the most part, even the slacker husbands weren't really *telling* us to clean. Brook had rarely asked me to pick up, except maybe my work clothes piled in the bedroom. This need for cleanliness was pressure I mostly put on myself. Brook just didn't care that much; his standards were lower. But this date reminded me how often he washed laundry, cleaned dishes, and wiped the table. Those were the types of messes he noticed, so he cleaned them without my prompting and often without my thanks. I realized I needed to acknowledge those contributions more consistently.

But for everything else, he just didn't share my perspective on what constituted a mess. We could look at the same floor and both see the same dried stain by the door, and while it cried out to me to be cleaned, Brook didn't even register a problem. Pointing it out made me a nag; cleaning it myself fostered resentment.

I'd hoped this date would somehow allow Brook to see our apartment and its messes as I did, that together we would come up with a solution that would free me from the shackles of chore stress. It had been a beautiful idea, but after ninety minutes of I-do-more-than-you back and forth, I considered this date a failure.

Sometimes it's depressing to realize your relationship is not a special snowflake. Almost every couple seems to have this same household fight, a battle many wage and no one seems to win. One friend's solution was to create a spreadsheet tracking time spent on household chores, hoping it would compel her husband to do more when he saw how little he contributed. Surprise, surprise, that didn't work! Another friend just accepted the 1950s option and did most of the housework since her live-in boyfriend had longer work hours and made more money. He didn't mind the arrangement, but she soon grew tired of it. The only option that really intrigued me came from a power couple who both worked demanding full-time jobs. She decided to lower her standards for how clean the house should be. And they got a cleaning lady.

And so, as we wrapped up this date, retreating quietly to opposite ends of the grimy apartment, stewing over how unappreciative our partner was, I came up with my plan. If household chores were always going to cause such tension, then I was going to minimize the chores that needed to be done. I was going to practice caring less about . . . *Who was I kidding, this wasn't going to make me feel any better.*

After a few minutes apart, Brook and I found ourselves back in the living room, standing next to that three-week-old stain. We hugged and I started to cry. "Okay, so I think there's one more thing I want to say," I managed to get out through the tears. "I hate that I think this. It's awful. But I feel this way and if I don't say this now I never will. I resent that I go to work every day and make most of our money, yet I do more of the housework. You work from home so I feel like you should take more of a lead on this."

I was as bad as the lazy hedge-fund husbands, expecting my boyfriend to clean the house because he made less money. But damn it, sometimes when I walked in the front door after a long day at the office or a stressful work trip and saw my boyfriend in a messy house clicking around on Twitter, I fumed. I never wanted to say anything, though, partly because it felt unfair and partly because I thought the roles might one day be reversed.

Brook tightened the hug. "Okay," he said.

I opened my eyes and peeked over his shoulder. The stain by the door didn't actually look so bad. Maybe it wasn't really the stain that upset me, otherwise I probably would have just cleaned it up. It would have taken all of one minute. The stain bothered me because it was a reminder that I still had trouble telling Brook what I wanted; I hoped he would just figure it out on his own. He wasn't going to improve as a mind reader, or probably as a housekeeper either, but we were finally getting better at expressing what we wanted.

When I came home from work the next day, the stain was gone. Brook had mopped and gone grocery shopping so he could make dinner. I hate to say it, but it was a lovely surprise.

DATE #23
_____

Play It Back

JILL: Halloween was eight months away, but Brook and I sat down on the couch to watch a scary movie. During our last date, we'd planned ahead for this one by filming ourselves doing "It's a Chore." Now we would "Play it Back" to see how we communicated during a fight. There we were, frozen on the screen, clutching our lists of household chores. Brook went to hit play, but I stopped him.

"I just want to say I love you and I'm going to keep an open mind as I watch this," I said. "I want to learn and make this easier in the future." He chuckled and we kissed. Hit play. Cue bloodbath.

But it wasn't what I expected. "I've divided the apartment into four areas," Brook began. Interesting. In my memory, the conversation was super confrontational from the moment it started. But watching it played back, it seemed almost pleasant for a while. I kept waiting for the moment we snapped, but there wasn't really one. We just slowly started drifting to a more combative tone.

Jill: We never sweep.

Brook: I do it probably once a week.

Jill: But not the whole floor, right?

On the TV I saw Brook's body language changing; he wasn't looking at me, he wasn't even really talking. But the Jill on the screen didn't seem to notice the descent into conflict. She still thought we were having a productive conversation. "Hey, do you think we've seen enough?" I asked Brook. He shook his head and kept watching. I slumped on the couch.

If I had to watch this I might as well learn something, so I pulled out my notebook. It was amazing how different the fight seemed when I wasn't in the middle of it. The first thing I noticed was that I was too wordy. Yes, I know, I know, all these dates seem to have this theme, but it was still shocking how unequal the conversation was. I easily said ten words for every one of his. The more I talked, the less Brook did. And rather than shutting up and letting him respond, I repeated what I'd said or explained it slightly differently. More words from me, more silence from him. When Brook did speak up, the moment he finished his thought I was back defending myself or disagreeing. Now in the video we were up off the couch, arguing about how the Tupperware was organized.

Jill: It's really very simple.

Brook: Then why can't I find any matching tops?

Jill: They're right in the damn cabinet.

Our disagreement progressed around the apartment—countertops, the bathroom, paperwork, spare coin storage. We were just talking past each other, getting angry at what we thought the other person was implying without actually making sure we understood each other's point. No wonder our apartment was back to being a mess.

BROOK: Finally the date on the TV finished. From the beginning, the main theme I noticed was Jill's barely contained frustration.

She was trying to be nice, but this was her big chance to say the things she usually held in. *I'm sounding like such a bitch right now but I've kept this inside for two years.*

Jill didn't like confrontation. As Noelle had warned me a while back, it was an Andres family trait. Every day there was stuff she was holding in, so when we finally had this formal discussion she had lots of pent-up ammo to shoot off. *Pow. Bang. Mop. Sweep.* At the time, for Jill, it felt like a real fireworks display, but on the tape it didn't look that bad to her. For me it was the opposite. I don't mind confrontation, so in the moment it didn't bother me. But watching us on tape, I felt like Jill came after me from the start. "Not confrontational?" I said. "Almost the first words out of your mouth were condescending, asking me if I noticed the mess on the floor from the leaky trash bag."

"That wasn't condescending," she said. "I was just mentioning something that I thought was a problem." We decided to watch that part of the tape again. I hit play and the Jill on TV said: "Our house is filthy, we actually have stains all over the floor. . . . So do you, like, not notice it?"

To me that sounded like: *You're such an idiot that you need a puddle of trash pointed out to you.*

"See, I'm not being condescending," she said. "You'd just told me you hadn't seen it, so I was pointing it out." Even after watching it twice she didn't hear it the way I heard it. That was pretty discouraging. On the screen I could see how outsiders would view us—the lazy guy and the nagging girl. Stock characters who wouldn't even get booked on Maury Povich. It was barely Steve Wilkos material. This was all stuff we could have found in any of the books we skimmed in the sculpture garden.

The devil was in the generalities, in how true the clichés could be. Yes, there were neat-freak guys and slobby girls; there were cheating women and snooping men. But more often we followed the same old, tired script we liked to believe we had evolved beyond.

Most women want their homes cleaner than most men. Men keep their feelings, about this and everything else, to themselves. And in a way that works out well for women. There's an upside to being silently judgmental while reminding yourself of all the things you do for the house that your boyfriend doesn't reciprocate. If she actually said it out loud she'd have to confront the fact that the stuff she prioritizes isn't stuff the two of them decided on together or stuff that he wanted, it's the stuff *she's* decided is important. By not reaching consensus, by not giving his preferences equal weight, she gets to privately set expectations and then privately blame him for not meeting them. The expectations are only mentioned implicitly when it comes time to point out that he isn't keeping up his end of a bargain he never entered into. (Wow, that felt good to say!)

But all of that gender dynamics stuff aside, even if I convinced Jill to want what I wanted in our home, that wouldn't solve the underlying issue of how we communicated. And the main thing I noticed when Jill and I fought was how we both treated each other like morons. The Tupperware thing was a classic example, a volley of increasingly passive-aggressive snark. It was easier to see when you could pause and rewind. It was even getting a bit easier to sense in the moment these days. If we could learn to identify that pattern and stop it before it went too far, maybe then things wouldn't get so messy.

Professional Advice

BROOK: In the span of an hour I made four trips to my closet, searching for something to wear. Nothing seemed right. Jill and I were going to couples counseling, and a sensible person would have understood that what he wore did not matter. But I was not in a sensible place. Going to couples counseling terrified me.

We've written a lot about testing Jill and Brook 2.0, but I've mainly glossed over *how* and *why* I came to that second relationship as a better guy. It's bleak, unpleasant stuff, and there's an instinct to package personal transformation into a snappy montage; the Navy SEAL training sequence in *American Sniper* takes up four minutes of a two-hour movie. Maybe it's more pleasant to believe we change through rapid magic than genuine anguish. Well, allow me a few honest, disagreeable paragraphs.

A couple of months after breaking up with Jill I'd slipped into the old pattern: casually dating lots of women, telling them we'd never be serious. None of them could hurt me because I didn't let any of them matter. Romantic love just seemed like something I wasn't capable of. It was the same feeling of certain, impending failure I had while dating Jill. I wasn't strong enough, or good enough, to make it work.

That was what sent me to therapy—the overwhelming sense that I couldn't be part of a real relationship. The fact I cheated on Jill wasn't the point. With enough willpower I could have been a faithful, lousy partner. But whether I physically strayed or not, that urge for endless, fresh validation kept my heart from ever really investing in one person. Cheating was the symptom that made the disease impossible to ignore.

So I went to therapy, and therapy sucked. It was the most brutal experience of my life. There were lots of sessions where I cried more in an hour than I had the previous thirty years. It made me feel no better. For long months I felt much worse. On the nights I slept alone I cried myself to sleep, swaddled in suicidal thoughts and soupy despair.

But I mention all this because the *how* and the *why* are important. I didn't become a better boyfriend because I loved Jill more or because I wanted more badly for it to work. I only became capable of being a better partner after surviving that brutal year, after reckoning with the hurt and insecurity I had always just numbed with the approval of women. I didn't find any shortcuts on that journey, and no one cheered a fucking step of it. At the end, at best, you got a skeptical nod—*Okay, it looks like you might meet the minimum requirements now.*

I wore jeans, my best shoes, and a dress shirt; Jill was already waiting in the reception area when I got there. In my experience, therapy was the place you went to learn awful things about yourself and I worried I'd discover Jill was wrong to give me another chance. It was hard to breathe.

"So why are you two here?" the therapist began. She sat in an antique chair cradling a yellow legal pad. It was a pretty foggy experience for me; I couldn't quite hear the words we were all saying or keep track of them, but I made sure to keep my arms unfolded so the therapist wouldn't critique my nonverbal communication. I spoke haltingly, almost clinically, about the history of our relationship, about the issues we had been dealing with, but I didn't get very far.

"Some couples come here as a way of breaking up," she said. "They don't know how to do it themselves, so they use the session as a way of doing it for them." I kept my arms uncrossed. "My sense is, that's not you two." She quickly pushed away from any specifics we had managed to mention and moved toward some general truths she already surmised: We took our relationship seriously and had been together a long time. "Nothing is perfect," she said.

This didn't feel like therapy. I expected agonizing introspection. This was more like a Dr. Phil pep rally. I wasn't sure what to make of it.

"If you wait for something perfect, you'll never take that leap," she said. "At some point you need to join hands and take that leap together and just work on your relationship as you go."

JILL: It felt to me like a moment of reckoning. "I guess the biggest fear I have left," I said hesitantly, "is that our old issues will come back." How could something so simple be so hard to say? I stared down at a dry tissue in my lap.

"Me too," Brook said. He reached across the couch and grabbed my hand.

"I sense that you both are pleasers," she said. "Pleasers are often afraid to hurt each other's feelings, so they don't express frustrations and disappointments."

The moment felt familiar. Probably because this wasn't Brook's and my first time sitting across from a therapist. Years before we'd been the desperate, weary couple asking for help, but as our new therapist had pointed out, in reality we were probably just using therapy to start letting go. We actually only made it through four tearful sessions; our fifth was scheduled for the morning after we broke up.

I went alone. Our counselor-turned-breakup-advisor let me cry and told me he knew I was going to be okay. He even offered an expert prediction: "In about a year, just as you're really starting to move on with someone else, Brook will try to get back together with you. You should prepare yourself for that moment."

I sort of laughed him off. "No, we're really through," I told him. But he'd been eerily right, almost to the day.

Before I left that post-breakup session and started my new life as single Jill Andres, I asked him if he thought Brook and I ever had a chance to "fix" our relationship. "Given your line of work, you must believe that people can change or else why would you bother?" I said. "But have you actually seen people change?"

He leaned back in silence for a second. "I have seen people change. Absolutely. But it takes lots and lots of hard work."

When Brook and I started dating again I thought quite a bit about those words and looked for signs of Brook's work and change. I found them. Brook hadn't just *said* he'd work on himself or visited a therapist a handful of times because someone asked. He had actually done the hard work to understand himself better. His emotional availability not only made him a better partner, it raised the bar for my own behavior. I had to change too. More than anything these dates took the measure of our growth.

"One problem we've had over the years is telling each other what's bothering us," I said to the new therapist, describing the first item I had put on my FYI List. But before she could even respond, it struck me that I was describing a concern from a different relationship. All we did now was talk about hard things! In just the last few dates we'd discussed my struggles with fitness and Brook's aversion to Windex. It had become awfully hard to complain about how much we shared. So I went ahead and did it—I mentally crossed off the first item on my FYI List right there on the couch. One red flag lowered.

Our hour was almost up but we had a final question: We wanted to know what the other couples who sat here dealt with. What were the most frequent issues facing her married clients?

"Well, the most common things are what you'd expect: sex, family, and finances. But the specifics are different for every couple; you can't really generalize. And a lot of times those things are superficially what the couple is fighting about, but in reality there's some deeper, unspoken conflict that is the real issue. It's really different with every couple."

The therapist asked if we wanted to come in for another session. I looked at Brook and he squeezed my hand. "No, I think we're good for now," I said. It felt like we were getting close to the edge of the diving board, and the two of us would have to look down alone and either turn back around or jump off together.

BROOK: It was cold outside when I left the therapist's office. Jill was a couple of minutes behind me, I think in the bathroom, and it was good to have a moment alone. I leaned back against the building and looked up at the sagging, snowy tree branches.

After we got back together I had told Jill almost everything about my time in therapy. But she could never fully know what happened. Her decision to give us another chance had not been rational, because odds were I hadn't really changed. Every lousy guy says he's changed. But Jill gave me another chance, which no rational person should do. She showed irrational faith in me, more faith than I had in myself sometimes. She never once brought up the past in anger; her forgiveness was the greatest act of love I'd ever experienced. Just thinking about that, standing alone under the snowy tree, made my eyes water.

"Ready?" she said. We held hands and put them in my pocket, walked toward home, and left that behind us.

Quality Time

❦

DATE #25

Blackout by Design

JILL: The name of the game was Stratego, and for over a year its unopened box had been wedged between an old Frisbee and a rarely used iron in our hall closet. But its fortunes had suddenly changed! Brook and I were cutting the digital cord for one workweek, and Stratego was suddenly, improbably, our top entertainment option—the apartment wasn't big enough to use the Frisbee. Since we still needed to do our jobs, the self-imposed blackout would run from 6 P.M. to 7 A.M. No phones, TVs, or computers; no stereos, e-readers, or iPods. We wanted to know how much of a drain (or crutch) our digital appetites were to our relationship. So that Monday we powered down all ten of our wireless-enabled devices and sat at our kitchen table applying a sticker to each Stratego piece.

Quality time is obviously important to any couple, but for Brook and me it had been the unmistakable foundation of our life together. We didn't begin as Facebook pen pals or hot and heavy lovers; we had started off as friends who could hang out for hours on end. Perhaps because we were friends before we added genders to the front of that title, we'd always had a lot of shared interests, and quality time seemed to happen organically.

And for most couples, time together is pretty much all high-quality at first—long romantic dinners, conversations about a shared love for Britney Spears's B-sides—after all, it's quality time that turns you into a couple.

But the more serious a relationship gets, the more the balance of time moves from quality to "other." Bills need to be paid, mothers need to be called, chores need to be done. The next thing you know, those enjoyable activities that enhance your relationship are being crowded out. If Brook and I made a life together, there would only be more things getting in the way (no offense, future children or employers). Already, the slippery slope between "quality time" and "other time" was a bit of a concern, so we decided to devote a whole series of activities to working on ways to improve the time we spent together.

What counts as quality time varies by couple. For us, just sitting together fantasizing about our next travel destination or debating some story in the news was quality time. I knew other couples with totally different tastes. One good friend and her girlfriend loved cleaning together. "It's cathartic!" she claimed. So they scheduled cleaning dates where they'd crank music and tidy as a team. Another grad school friend hosted Sunday night pizza parties with her husband, treating a few lucky neighbors to homemade pies featuring veggies they grew together in their garden.

The tricky thing for couples was remembering that time together did not equal quality time. And as if bills and mothers weren't enough, most of us were taking a third wheel on virtually all our dates, a slender if boxy companion that stole much of our attention. I'd like to think I'm fun to talk to, but it's hard to compete with all of humanity's collected knowledge. Electronics were probably the number one enemy of our quality time. It annoyed Brook that I read my phone in bed; I didn't understand how he could look at Twitter every hour of the day.

At our kitchen table that Monday night, we spent two hours just playing a board game, just the two of us. I don't know the last time we'd been so cut off from the rest of the world. Even traveling to the ends of the earth often wasn't enough to get this kind of digital peace and quiet; I'd stayed in bamboo huts with no running water but uninterrupted WiFi. We finished our Stratego game, put all the pieces back in the box, and had sex for a really long time. Bliss.

BROOK: True, first thing in the morning I grabbed my phone and checked e-mail—I hadn't signed up to be Amish. But I looked forward to six o'clock—there was something freeing about the blackout. I was one of the last people I knew to get a smartphone because I'd been afraid it would take over my life. And I was right, it totally had; I was on my damn phone *all* the time and didn't have the willpower to stop.

I felt especially crummy about it because disconnecting had actually been a kind of important part of my identity. One reason I was always a good budget traveler was that I could happily sit on a bus for eight or ten hours and just let my mind wander; killing time without help was the closest thing I ever had to a superpower. But I no longer had those long introspective stretches, and I sensed that made me less creative, maybe even less intelligent in a way. It almost certainly made me a worse boyfriend. Every slow moment had become a reason to check Twitter.

"Hey, babe." Jill came home after work Tuesday, and that was my cue to close my laptop. Very quickly our world felt slower and quieter and smaller in a good way—like moving from a sold-out cruise ship to a remote château. The weather was bad so we stayed in, and as we played cards, my hand unconsciously fingered the left pocket of my jeans. I finally noticed it groping for my phone and directed it back above the table to hold my cards. But every time I lost focus on the game I would awake to find my left hand exploring that pocket. Username: Pavlov. Password: Zuckerberg.

We could only play cards for so long, and eventually we had to settle for another long night of sex. If I were a sex therapist my whole regime would be making my patients turn off their phones. It does wonders. If I were a sleep therapist I would offer the same prescription. I'm not a good sleeper but this week it was easy. By 10 P.M. we both drifted off peacefully.

I must, however, report a logistical drawback to the digitally ascetic lifestyle. On Wednesday, Jill had a work dinner and we planned to meet for a drink afterward. I showed up alone to the bar downstairs from her restaurant and jockeyed for a place to watch *SportsCenter*—a questionable bending of the rules. Ten minutes passed and then thirty and then an hour. No Jill. No way to get in touch with her. Finally she appeared at the bar. "I'm so sorry, dinner is running really late, we just got our food." I wasn't mad *at* Jill, exactly, but the situation was annoying and she was the reason I was caught up in it. I sipped my drink for another half hour. Standing there without anything to do kind of sucked, but it gave me the longest stretch alone with my thoughts in a very long time, a chance to mentally wander without any real goals or distractions. That part was nice.

At the end of the week, sitting at a high-top table with friends, I felt my hand caress my jeans. It was happening less often than at the beginning of the week, but it still happened. It was a signal that my attention was drifting, a reminder to stay in the moment. During the whole Marriage Test I don't think we'd done another activity more personally worthwhile than this one.

<hr>

DATE #26

Time Well Spent

BROOK: At some point Jill reminded me that we were going to start a date called "Time Well Spent." The idea was to keep track of what we did every day for two weeks and then look back at our records and think about which activities were rewarding and which weren't. Then we could make an effort to increase the things we valued and cut out the stuff that was just filling space.

I thought it was a good idea. It sounded a bit like a food journal. We all know we eat some good food and some junk food, but our brain can play tricks with how much of each we actually have. When you write down every apple and every slice of pizza, the totals can be different than you imagined. And what about that plate of pasta or avocado or eggplant parm? When you run the numbers, their impact on your diet can be surprising. Or so I'd heard. I'd never actually *done* a food journal, but I would do this "Time Well Spent" thing and strengthen my relationship!

But Jill was going away on a business trip at the end of the week and then I was going out of town, so we had to put it off for a while. And then our schedules really got hectic and I wondered when we were ever going to find time to keep track of our time, so I asked Jill what the plan was.

"You haven't been doing the date?" she said. "We decided last Sunday that we would start it the next day. This was the only time we had to do it. I've been keeping track."

"Oh. I didn't think that was what we said. I thought we said we wanted to start but we couldn't because we were both out of town part of the week. Maybe I have some notes in my e-mail. Let me take a look; I'll try to reconstruct something." But I didn't. For the first time, I had straight-up failed a date.

JILL: When I arrived home the first night of "Time Well Spent," it looked like Brook had already started the date. The apartment was the cleanest I'd ever seen it, and dinner simmered on the stove. Ever since finishing "It's a Chore," this was happening more and more often, a very welcome change. We squeezed in a workout and some alone time before eating together and relaxing on the couch. Dessert was served in bed.

It was all quality time, I wrote in my journal the next morning. *He made me feel so special and we got shit done!*

Night one was so strong I suspected Brook might have planned it that way, trying to ace "Time Well Spent." So I was totally surprised when I learned later that he'd forgotten to start the date. It was all organic quality time? I hadn't expected such harmony when we conceived of this activity months before on our Potomac kayaking trip. I figured the date would just rekindle the "we spend too much time together" argument . . . and probably prove again that Brook was right. We lived in the same small apartment; the date was certain to show that we saw a lot of each other.

Before we started this project I thought this ongoing tension came from the sheer number of hours we spent together. But our "Can't Touch This" blowup actually reframed the problem for me. I realized I'd misunderstood what we were fighting about all these years. Yes, we spent a lot of time together, but Brook's main complaint was that when we were together I demanded almost all his attention. I wanted to talk, be entertained, interact . . . and sometimes he just needed me to be a quiet, unobtrusive presence when we were near one another. As my FYI List reminded me, *I can be overbearing.*

I thought a lot about this after our fight and had tried to keep tabs on myself over the last few months. After all, this was the one FYI item entirely under my control. I alone had to learn how to satisfy my need for interaction without always relying on Brook to provide it. So the "Time Well Spent" date gave me a chance to really track my progress. Yes, it confirmed how much time we spent together. During four of the five nights, we interacted only with each other. But what was different this week versus months before was that I wasn't actively engaging him whenever we were together. On Wednesday, when I got home from work and Brook was still busy editing video, I happily kept to myself.

Having time to take care of the things I needed to do even though he was home was really good, I noted in my journal. The next night I went out with a friend for dinner and Brook elected to stay home. When I returned, he'd finished his work and was ready to pay attention to me. We gave each other massages. This was the kind of quality time we needed.

"Time Well Spent" felt like proof that we were making progress. Even the fact that Brook forgot to start the date seemed like a good sign. If my overwhelming personality really was such a big deal, he would have been jumping at the chance to show me the facts. Instead, it wasn't enough of a priority for him to even remember to do it.

So on day five, when I learned I was the only one evaluating our "Time Well Spent," I actually considered the date a success. I'd collected enough evidence to take a big step. I crossed *I can be overbearing* off my FYI List in bold red pen. I knew this wasn't the last time we'd talk about how chatty I was or how much time we spent together, but I finally really understood his frustrations, noticed when I was starting to be overbearing, and had ways to minimize the tension.

And there was something else that jumped out as I skimmed through my notes from the week—I almost didn't believe it. Monday: *had sex.* Tuesday: *hooked up again.* Wednesday: *came home, hooked up right away.* Thursday: *fun, different sex.* Friday: *sex again. Who were we?*

My FYI List had *Are we sexually compatible?* underlined and encircled with sad faces. Did we really just have sex five nights in a row without noticing? It was like keeping a food journal and discovering you only ate vegetables. That *never* happens. But it had just happened to us. While we weren't paying attention, we'd naturally developed a super-strong and healthy sexual connection. In a truly bullish moment I regripped the red pen. Sex might not stay like this for fifty years—it almost certainly wouldn't—but I believed we'd established a natural spark of sexual compatibility and had the tools to keep that fire alive over time. I crossed *sex* off my list too.

For a failed date, it sure pointed to a lot of progress.

That night, I showed Brook my notes and finally told him about the nearly empty FYI List. It had started to feel strange keeping something so central to this project from him. He looked it over intently.

"Wow, this couple has come a long way," he said, smiling. "They discuss their problems now, they're too busy hooking up to talk all the time. They should write a book."

"No way, too much work, they're having it auto-written."

At the bottom of the page, there was one item still on the list, the pressure I felt to work out. Brook didn't mention it.

You're in Charge

BROOK: I hadn't read *Fifty Shades of Grey*, but I felt a bit like the intense guy I saw in the movie trailer. I was on my phone, typing out instructions to Jill, who, for a day, had to do whatever I told her. The idea of "You're in Charge" was to take turns pushing the other to live the way we wished they would.

Not long before, Jill had shown me her FYI List and beamed as she explained all the concerns she'd crossed off. I felt good about us too, confident enough to head into a stressful date without shying away from where it might lead.

I figured Jill would make me mop for most of the day she was in charge, and she assumed I would "just have her go running for seven hours," or "lock her in a gym all day." In the lead-up to the date she made constant jokes about me making her work out, and they weren't fun to hear. No one wants to be the guy asking his girlfriend to work out more. Everyone hates that guy. That's why I had gone the better part of a decade not saying anything about exercise. And yet, according to her FYI List, pressure to work out was her biggest remaining concern about our future. Was I some *Maxim*-programmed dude-bro giving his girlfriend body image issues? For a while I worried I might be.

And then I stumbled into a funny conversation at a friend's bachelor party. I was surrounded by four married guys, and all four of them began commiserating about being hassled to work out by their fitness-focused wives. "She slaps me on the gut every time she goes for a run," one of them joked. It wasn't a man-vs.-woman thing, it was an active-partner-vs.-less-active-partner thing. Once more, we were not special snowflakes.

The night before "You're in Charge," I wrote some simple instructions to Jill. I was jammed up on a story in New York, too busy to sort the details myself and not due home until the next evening. *For tomorrow, make a reservation for this 7 a.m. yoga class.* What red-blooded young woman doesn't enjoy yoga? She wrote back that all of the morning yoga classes in D.C. were full. *What about this?* she wrote, with a link to some kind of yuppy, girly workout class where they swing a bar around and do leg kicks. It sounded fine to me.

There were a few other habits I hoped to encourage in Jill. *Bring a yogurt and apple to work and consume both at 4:30 p.m.*, I wrote. Jill constantly walked in the door hungry, making her a bit cranky and forcing me to eat an early dinner. And Jill liked to paint but never did. *After work, please proceed to Utrecht art store and purchase $20–$50 of art supplies to work with tonight.*

JILL: My marching orders were clear. After getting up at 5:45 A.M., exercising and working a full day, I would shop for art supplies, paint, and then have dinner waiting for Brook's 9:00 P.M. arrival home. He said to take a nap if I wanted, but didn't leave me time to do it. I was a little surprised by how much energy he expected me to have. But, hey, this was his chance to be in charge and show me how he wished I lived my life, so I drank a late-afternoon black tea and dove into my assignments. It felt novel to just shut up and do what I was told for once. (I hoped Brook wasn't going to get used to this.)

One thing I'd always appreciated about Brook was what a great influence he was on me. Yeah, he wanted me to work out more and for a million reasons that was complicated, but otherwise he was a really positive, gentle force. When I wasn't sure about going to grad school, he was encouraging without making me feel pressured. When I had a problem with my foot, he wouldn't let me just ignore the pain and kept my spirits up as treatment after treatment failed. He even got me to start flossing! I knew he had my best interest at heart, and this "You're in Charge" date was no exception.

As I strolled through the art store aisles, I started feeling inspired. I wasn't an especially talented painter, but I enjoyed playing around with color and texture. When I moved to D.C., my paints and brushes fell victim to a too-small moving van, so it had been nearly two years since I flexed those creative muscles. I ended up spending $23.46 on new acrylic paints, three brushes, and two small canvases. I wasn't sure what I was going to do, but I found myself hurrying home to get started.

When Brook walked in a few hours later, I greeted him holding my latest creation: a small green, white, and black portrait of Stone "Enjoy By" IPA, our favorite beer. It seemed like a fun way to practice lettering and I thought he'd find it funny. There was a pretty pathetic pot of pasta on the stove, but in my defense I got caught up painting and had to race to get dinner done.

I felt really satisfied with my day as it was, but Brook had one last surprise. After dinner, we rushed out of the apartment to catch a show at Black Cat, a music venue near our house, arriving just as the main act started. I had spent a lot of nights at Black Cat during my first stint in D.C. after college; now it was a place I mostly just

walked by, promising myself I'd go sometime soon. The show was
nothing special, but it was fun to be there with Brook and reminisce
about all the crazy times my friends and I had spent there.

That night, as I got ready for bed I thought, *Damn, I got a lot done
today, that's how I should live most days!* I'm not sure Brook planned it
that way, but the day was focused on things I always talked about but
rarely got around to doing. I had probably set my alarm for an early
workout 100 times, but this was the first morning I actually did it.
And it was great!

~ ⁂ ~

A couple of days later it was my turn to wear the bossy pants. (They
fit perfectly, har har.) While Brook's plans had nudged me toward
positive activities, my plans were designed to help him manage his
stressful workload. He was in the middle of wrapping up a huge
editing project and I could see the toll his long hours were taking. It
was my turn to be a positive influence.

The night before, I gave him just two "tasks" for the morning:
Don't set an alarm and *Stretch for ten minutes before turning on your computer
or phone.* I was such a great girlfriend! Had I known that my day was
going to start at 5:45 A.M., I might have planned his a little differently.
When I left for work the next morning, Brook was sleeping peacefully. I e-mailed him an overview of the rest of his responsibilities:
*Eat breakfast within an hour of waking up (poached eggs and bread), drink
three pints of water, go grocery shopping, at 5 p.m. work out for an hour, pack for
NYC, take the metro to our softball game so you can walk home with me after,
hook up with me before we fall asleep).*

For the most part I just wanted him to remember to do the little
things that made him feel better and less stressed. When I compared how I bossed him to how he bossed me, I noticed that I really

didn't push him very far out of his comfort zone, aside from getting groceries. For the most part I ordered him to do things he tended to already do. Maybe I'm not quite as bossy as everyone says I am!

BROOK: I watched the clock, making sure to stretch for the full ten minutes, which actually took a lot of willpower. I meant to stretch every morning but always reached for my phone and started reading e-mails and next thing I knew it was dinnertime. So Jill was a good influence. But even as a boss she was really nonconfrontational. Her instructions consisted of "demands" such as *Sleep in!*

Eventually I realized this date was a microcosm of our nonverbal communication styles. Jill hated being told what to do, so she set a good example by not telling me what to do. She might take the lead with her big personality, but she never really complained about anything I did, which made it harder for me to ask her for things.

But the structure of this date, and a bunch of other dates before it, forced her a bit out of those habits. When we discussed chores she finally let loose with her complaints about the mop and broom. And when she got a chance to boss me around she made at least one real demand: *Get groceries.* She did most of our grocery shopping and I knew she resented that.

But Jill wasn't going to ask for much and she wasn't going to ask loudly. If I wanted to I could brush off or pretend not to hear what she asked for because her requests would be subtle and infrequent. Of course her subtlety didn't mean she didn't care, just that she couldn't bring herself to shout it out, at least not before it reached the point of anger and utter frustration. I would have to listen and pay attention, treating her jokes and asides the way I might treat someone else's foot-stomping tantrums. Jill's way was a lot more pleasant than the foot-stomping-tantrum style. But it required better hearing and the self-discipline to listen to things I might not want to understand.

DATE #28

Your Ideal Day

BROOK: What did I really know about my girlfriend's desires? What did she know about mine? It was kind of the fundamental test of any relationship—to understand what makes the other person happy. So Jill set out to give me an "Ideal Day."

I already thought of our relationship as a constellation of great times. Most of the best moments of my life involved Jill ... drinking moonshine with a Chinese singing troupe; falling through a half-frozen New Hampshire river, then warming our damaged skin by the fire; accidentally driving our car up a pedestrian hiking path in France and having a picnic with Burgundy stretched out below us. Those days were unplanned adventures, but they weren't quite accidents, they were the product of pushing each other out of our homes and into the world. More than anything else, that was what Jill and I did so well together. Still, it would be hard to create an "Ideal Day" on command.

Just after 10 A.M., Jill had us hop on our bikes and ride south through D.C., stopping at Paul, the French bakery that supplied our picnics when Burgundy was too far a ride. We brought our snacks to a sunny stretch of grass right below the Washington Monument and as the tourists hurried by she pulled out a stack of newspapers and magazines, a pile of stories to read and discuss. Eventually we biked back to the sculpture garden and got a coffee, then pedaled down to the water in Georgetown. We were at the Potomac to go kayaking again.

We paddled out in the same direction we had six months before, away from the city. I recognized the cluster of trees growing improbably in the middle of the river on tiny islands of rocks; it was the spot where we came up with this project. We had done a slow circle around them as the first burst of date ideas came to us. I remember how fresh and exciting and novel the dates felt at the time. Now they seemed much smaller, like we had grown beyond swapping phones and credit cards. There was more light left in the day than there had been on our first trip, so we paddled much farther up the river, knowing we could coast home with the current.

"While we're back in this place I feel like we should talk about what fears we still have," I said. Just introducing the topic felt like a success. The words came out pretty easily. The point of the dates, and the focus of our relationship, seemed to be shifting. We spent less time now thinking about whether we should be together, and more time talking about how to make it as good as possible. The picture of our life together hadn't changed much, it had just become clearer. Fewer, *Yeah, buts*. More believable answers to how we'd overcome the stuff we struggled with.

But I still had fears. I worried about the one day every few months that reminded me of the old times, when Jill felt like an anchor, and the approval of some flirty girl had this familiar power. Admitting that ember of doubt made me feel like a failure. I couldn't bring myself to say it so bluntly to Jill. I guess I admitted as much as I thought I could without hurting her too badly. But I think what I wanted to confess was that any claim of certainty would be a lie; I would never be perfect, the future would never be certain.

We pulled up to the dock and found a big bill for the rental; we had been out there much longer than we realized.

JILL: The kayak chat didn't scare me. After twenty-eight dates, it felt natural to be open with each other. It actually comforted me that we could talk about temptation so frankly. Discussing those fears made me feel even closer to Brook. No more stomachaches and overanalysis.

But my plan for the end of Brook's ideal day was a bit risky. We were going to cook dinner together. Something about our personalities had always made collaborating in the kitchen especially difficult, so we had just stopped trying years before. Instead, we took turns cooking alone, because even assisting each other (*Let me do the rice*) led to tension (*You aren't going to put that much water in the rice, are you?*). Tonight we would step into the kitchen together as co-chefs, equals. I'd gone out the day before and procured the ingredients for steak au poivre, a pepper steak we liked but had never tried cooking.

We set off seasoning, chopping, and mixing. No assigned roles, we just rotated onto different tasks as needed. Brook's natural attention to detail meant he read the recipe, checked the clock, and prepared the sauce. I managed the prep and the grilling. As we glided around the kitchen together we actually felt in sync. Really, genuinely, truly happy. Brook snuck kisses in between steps in the recipe. The meat and sides done, we opened a bottle of wine we'd been saving, lit some candles I found deep in a kitchen drawer, and savored our tenderly prepared steak.

I know cooking is a small thing, but the meal was a sort of milestone. After years of not even trying to cook together because we were always stepping on each other's toes, we discovered it was

something we could now do. It was as if we'd developed a new power
without even realizing it.

Not knowing how the kitchen session would go, I had planned a
finale my man was sure to like: March Madness basketball and full-
body massage. I had him lie down in front of the TV and for the next
hour I worked out all his knots and tension. It may have been Brook's
ideal day, but when I went to bed that night I have to say it had been
great for me too.

~ ℯ ~

The ideal day Brook planned for me began one Saturday morning
on an air mattress in Queens. We let out the air, pushed it into the
corner of Jason and Deb's living room, and took the Q train into
Manhattan, munching on a pint of blueberries.

Brook didn't mention at first that this was my ideal day, but I could
tell that it would be fun; he said we were meeting friends in Central
Park. We strolled hand in hand into the overcrowded southern end of
the park, past the tour bus hawkers, hot dog carts, and T-shirt ven-
dors. We stepped over the manure-covered carriage route and looked
up at the passing tourists who were $90 poorer for the privilege of
sitting in a horse-drawn traffic jam that reeked of poop. Classic,
romantic Gotham.

Brook and I walked farther north into the park, to *our* Central
Park. We strolled by Sheep's Meadow, where we'd spent all those
summer weekends playing volleyball and people watching, then
over to the little performance space where street acrobats hyped up
the crowd in anticipation of a show that never seemed to actually
start, then walked to the open stretch of concrete where roller skat-
ers danced to seventies funk and soul.

Brook spotted a secluded hill and suggested we scamper up it.

What a view! To our left, we could see the pond at the southern edge of the park framed by the Midtown skyline. To our right, Belvedere castle and the Upper West Side, our old neighborhood. And straight below us, the twisted walking path halfway between my old office and his old apartment, the route I took to our first nights together.

"Hey, will you take a quick photo of me?" Brook asked. Even he was impressed by the view, he *never* asked for pictures of himself.

"Sure," I said, jumping up with my phone. "Okay, I'm taking a panorama so bear with me." I glided the phone 180 degrees from my left to right, Brook standing in the middle, hands in his pockets, with a wry smile. I finished to his left, pointing toward the two junior high school girls we were sharing the hill with, and spent a moment admiring my work, but when I turned to show Brook, he was gone. I looked right and left, confused. Then I spotted him below me; he seemed to have found something on the ground. I walked over to see what he was looking at.

"Jill, will you spend the rest of your life with me?"

He was on one knee, a ring in his hands, looking into my eyes. Time. Completely. Stopped.

I was suddenly kneeling on the ground next to Brook, crying, hugging him. Through the tears I somehow remembered to say, "Yes."

"I was afraid you might say, '*Yes, and . . .*'" Brook smiled.

We kissed and laughed; we looked at the ring. On. My. Finger. It fit perfectly. It was the most surreal moment of my life. I had a fucking diamond on my hand and Brook was going to be my husband! What the hell just happened?

"But what about the rest of our dates?" I asked, still out of breath.

Brook laughed. "I've thought about it; don't worry."

His proposal took me completely by surprise. For all the time we'd spent analyzing our relationship, I hadn't spent any time imaging this moment. I visualized us together, married, but I never actually pictured us getting engaged—we still had twelve more dates to finish! I didn't know what we were supposed to do now besides smile and kiss. So that was what we did. The two teenage girls were still there, giggling and wiping away tears themselves.

"Should we call our parents?" Brook asked. With a shaking thumb I dialed my mom and dad and put them on speakerphone. "Brook and I are in Central Park right now and he just asked me to marry him. I said yes, we're engaged!" They were thrilled; my dad went so far as to claim that he'd expected this even when we'd broken up. "That's why we wanted to stay in touch with you, Brook; you and Jill broken up just didn't make any sense!" We hung up and called Brook's family. "Oh my God!" screamed Brook's mom. "Holy crackers!"

We were both giddy with nervous excitement and I was still shaking from the adrenaline. "I've got some other surprises planned for us today," Brook said. He led us out of the park and across the street to the Time Warner Center. At the top of the escalators he opened a backpack I'd hardly noticed he was carrying and pulled out a slightly rumpled sport coat and fancy black dress.

"We have reservations at Per Se in five minutes," he said.

I tried to fix my hair in the reflection of the brass sign at the entrance of the restaurant. "Congratulations," the hostess said as she took the ratty coat I'd put on that morning, when my plans for the day, and our life, had felt very different.

Staring down at Central Park from our table, I could just about see the hill where we had been a half hour before. I was a girl who thought she wouldn't want a proper engagement ring; it would be too fancy and make me feel uncomfortable. But Brook had picked out a gorgeous and unique band made of small, overlapping leaves pointing up to a stunning diamond. It made me feel beautiful.

I asked Brook about it. "Well, remember when I was in Arkansas for work that week? I wasn't working. I found a place that lets you dig for your own diamonds. So I spent seven days shoveling dirt trying to find your diamond." That was the most Brook thing Brook had ever done.

"So you dug this up yourself?" I cried.

"Well, no . . . I spent seven days unsuccessfully digging for a diamond. I finally had to come back and just buy one."

We were both too keyed up to really appreciate the food, but the three-hour lunch was beautiful, uninterrupted time for the two of us. No cell phones or friends, just Brook and me, and this shiny thing on my hand. I couldn't believe it was happening.

Brook's original excuse for taking me to New York had been to celebrate his birthday, and he had asked our friends to clear their calendars. *I'm excited to announce tonight's birthday party was a ruse*, he e-mailed the group after lunch. *We'll actually be celebrating our engagement this evening in room 4305 of the London Hotel.*

I loved surprises and this most "ideal day" was full of them. On the walk from lunch to the hotel we stopped into Whole Foods, where he had reserved a case of "Enjoy By" IPA, that favorite beer I had painted a couple of dates before.

Our glass-walled room hovered above the city; the view was incredible and we were finally alone and soon all over each other, rough and passionate. It felt like we were hooking up for the first time. "It's just you and me now," he whispered as we lay next to each other. He hugged me so tight. He looked happier than I could ever remember seeing him. I wish I were a good enough writer to express what his happiness did to my heart.

BROOK: Relief. I guess first it was relief. I hadn't worried whether she'd say yes; I really felt we were both ready. But relief that the uncertainly was over, that we would be together, that I hadn't lost her—that was probably the biggest thing I felt.

But I'd also spent the last month stressed about the logistics of the day—getting the restaurant reservation, finding a place for the party, worrying about the weather. I spent a month with this secret I shared with no one because I wanted her to be the first to know. The ring had been in my middle dresser drawer, folded into a pair of sweatpants. Every day I pulled it out of the case when she was at work. It made our problems seem tiny, the fights seem silly. Jill would get upset about something and I'd want to say, "Babe, this doesn't matter, we're going to spend our lives together."

The hotel suite started to fill up. My family were the first ones to knock; I had asked them to drive down from Rhode Island for my birthday, so they were already on their way when we called with the news. "I was afraid you'd never find anyone," my mom sobbed, the way only a mom can sob.

Jason, who had played *Brook* as a vain but decent guy eleven dates before, came in with a bottle of André sparkling wine. Katie, the friend who had introduced us in Boston, arrived with a bottle of Moët. (If you ever have an engagement party, don't buy champagne; everyone else will bring it.) The room turned pink with the sunset and got loud with the voices of all the friends who had filled out our survey, those who said we were "a great match," as well as those who thought we were "good enough, I guess."

My friend Craig carried in the heavy tin tray I'd asked him to pick up downtown. Dinner in the hotel suite was tacos from Zaragoza. We had first discovered Zaragoza because their ceiling also served as the floor of Jill's shitty apartment on Avenue A. When we started telling people about the amazing $2 tacos served from a bodega hot plate, we joked that they weren't allowed to tell anyone else or the place would be ruined by popularity. After Jill moved out of the apartment, the *New York Times* did a story on Zaragoza and the tacos went up to $3.50 and friends said the food, now popular, wasn't as good as it used to be. But Jill and I still liked it. Those stupid tacos explained as well as anything why I was so excited to spend my life with Jill.

I had never met anyone with Jill's combination of talent and taste—the ability to achieve material success and the good judgment to understand what was truly valuable in life. Hard work and good luck would probably give us financially comfortable lives, but knowing we'd be together meant that wouldn't matter. With her, dinner from Zaragoza was as good as lunch at Per Se. Dusk in the hotel penthouse could be traded for sunrise in a thatch hut. The things we liked could be popular or played out; we could fly to Europe or paddle on the Potomac. I really believed we'd feel rich and young for as long as we were together.

Around 2 A.M. we kicked out the stragglers. In the morning I woke up next to Jill for the first time knowing I would wake up next to her forever.

Partnership

Road Trip Packing List

BROOK: Deodorant, some underwear, maybe two bras? What about tampons, did I need tampons? Our first date as an engaged couple was taking us on a road trip to Florida. The challenge was packing, not for ourselves, but for each other, without asking for help and without a chance to go back and get what we forgot. It was a three-day trip, so that meant like half a dozen tampons? Where did she even keep them?

There were two reasons I decided to propose to Jill before we finished the forty dates. The first was simply that I thought we were ready, and I'd begun to feel that the dates were holding us back from moving forward with our lives. But the second reason was something I saw in Florida a month before.

My grandfather was in the hospital, his lungs surrounded by

fluid, and freelancing gave me the flexibility to fly down to Tampa and hang out with him for a while. He was ninety-two and physically frail, but still wonderfully sharp. We talked baseball and family history and politics. He knew endless stuff you couldn't Google—the bad decision that got a certain baseball manager fired in the forties, the forgotten way FDR pronounced his own name (Ruse-evelt, not Rose-evelt).

My grandfather Arthur Silva had spent almost seventy years married. Fifty-one years with my grandmother and then, after her death, fifteen years and counting with his second wife; two marriages more successful than many people's best effort. Imagine how good you are at being married after seven decades' practice! It seemed like it should almost be easy. But then there was the issue of the phone.

Papa asked me to look through his papers for a phone bill. It had come just before he went into the hospital and seemed to charge him for service he never ordered. He didn't even have a phone plugged into the wall. So I asked his wife to bring the bill from home, and then everyone's story got very confusing.

Eighty-eight years old herself, she couldn't work the cell phone her son had given her. So maybe she went and ordered a landline behind my grandfather's back. She wasn't saying, maybe because she couldn't remember. There was a lot now she couldn't remember, and the worst part was she knew her mind was deserting her, and hated herself for it. My grandfather became enraged by these bills, delivered to a house he couldn't return to. His wife was clearly crushed by her inability to communicate her jumbled thoughts. Even with all those years of practice, being married couldn't have been harder.

As I sat with my grandfather, I thought about Jill. We had started these dates as a means of making a decision, as a long trip to a difficult destination. In his hospital room I realized there was no destination; our decision to marry just poured the foundation of a house we'd always be fixing. These months before the wedding would be a special moment in time when we knew we'd spend our lives together but hadn't yet formed the habits that would define us as a married couple. This was our chance to build a sturdy house. In a way, these would be our most important dates.

Even though we had been dating a long time, getting engaged stirred up strong and surprising emotions. I became overwhelmed by a thought that had never occurred to me before: Our relationship wasn't going to end by breaking up, it was going to end by one of us dying. I know that's an obvious and unromantic thing to say, but I couldn't shake it from my mind.

Happily, that morbid thought was balanced by a little piece of engagement magic: When you're dating someone, you're constantly subconsciously asking yourself, "Will this last?" It's the question at the core of every fight and every special moment. It's why dating someone seriously can feel so heavy, while being with someone who's leaving town at the end of summer is so damn simple. But a funny thing happened in the moment Jill said, "Yes." She became that breezy girl. I didn't have to worry where it was going. The "Will this last?" filter was gone and I felt an easy closeness to her that was entirely new.

Now we were going to Florida to retrieve my grandfather's car. He and his wife needed to fly up to Rhode Island so their families could take care of them. So Jill and I, on the opposite end of our lifetime together, would drive their Toyota fifteen hundred miles up I-95. Three pairs of socks, two tank tops, and a sweater. Oh, and her toiletry bag!

JILL: Brook volunteered to make the trip, but clearly it was too much driving for one person so I offered to join him. It was bad timing because one of my best friends was having her bachelorette party that weekend. (I had already RSVPed: "Yes, bring on the penis straws!"). But when I called to say I couldn't come, she agreed. "Jill, that's what we have to do now that we're getting married. Our fiancés take priority."

Fiancé, what a weird word. Or, was it *fiancée*? The night we got engaged I'd learned there was a difference but then promptly forgot what it was. But that's who Brook was now: my future husband.

Because they're usually the ones popping the question, guys have time before the engagement to prepare emotionally (and probably freak out a little). But it's different for the gals: The shift happens in one unexpected moment. You're taking a stroll or having dinner and—BOOM!—your life changes. I awoke one morning unsure if Brook and I would end up together and fell asleep that night in the arms of the man who promised to be there through thick and thin. What a Saturday! No wonder it took some time to sink in; how comforting that every day it felt even more *right*.

Really, the only awkward part was getting used to this word. *Fiancée*. No, wait, *fiancé*. You can talk about a boyfriend or husband without demanding attention, but mention your *fiancé* and you've humble-bragged into a surefire chance to tell the world about your precious, special love. I felt kind of icky just saying the word.

But like any good humble-brag, it seemed necessary to say. Brook and I had long ago outgrown the *boyfriend/girlfriend* title—we lived together, we were making life decisions together, we were starting to merge our finances. "My *partner* Brook" sounded like I was in a same-sex relationship or that we'd taken some strong stand against marriage. So we'd stuck with *boyfriend/girlfriend* right up until our moment in Central Park. Now, we finally had a label that fully described our commitment, but saying the f-word still felt so pretentious.

Whatever you called him, I was packing his bag and he was trying to pack mine. We'd planned these *Partnership* dates long before we got engaged, but they seemed so perfectly fitting now. Instead of testing compatibility, the remaining dates became a chance to strengthen our relationship and work out any remaining kinks before the "I do's." And since this was our first post-engagement date, I wanted to nail it.

Other couples could probably pack for each other by loading all their worldly possessions into several suitcases, but that would not fly in the newly created Andres/Silva-Braga household. Brook and I both prided ourselves on efficient, even ruthless packing. On my last three-month trip I'd brought less than twenty pounds of stuff. Brook lived out of a backpack for a year with just five pounds of clothes. We both believe you don't need much when you bring the *right* things. So every item I packed for him would have to be carefully selected.

I first collected Brook's basics—clothes, toiletries, chargers—and even managed to remember some less obvious things like contact lens cleaner and a bathing suit (just in case!). I stuffed Brook's allergy medication and one nice shirt into his pack and zipped it shut. It looked pretty much like it normally did when he packed. *Success?*

After work the next night we flew down to Tampa. We found his grandpa's car waiting for us in the parking lot, got in, and started driving north. Around 1 A.M. we pulled into a Jacksonville hotel and anxiously unzipped our bags. Brook went first.

"Really?" he said, holding up a shirt and shorts. "Have you ever seen me wear these things together?" He had a point. It was actually cute to hear him talk about some of his fashion preferences; overall we agreed I did pretty well. Then my clothes tumbled out. I noticed some things I wouldn't normally pack ("bedroom bras," if you know what I mean), but everything in the bag fit, went together, and made sense in the context of what we were doing. It was sort of interesting to see what he included—it suggested which items he wished I wore more often. That was an unexpected bonus.

So Brook aced the clothes portion of the test. But when I dumped out my bag looking for the rest of my stuff, not much of it was there. He hadn't bothered to review the contents of my toiletry bag, and it was missing a toothbrush, deodorant, face lotion, and makeup. He was lucky to have such a low-maintenance fiancé. I mean, fiancée. He also forgot to pack my birth control. I joked that he must be ready to start a family, but in true Andres form that joke just covered up my considerable irritation. He'd seen me take that pill every day for years and then it just didn't occur to him to pack it? He also forgot my phone charger, aka the item we'd need to power our navigation device. I just . . . I didn't really know what to say. He totally nailed the clothes—which can be really hard when packing for a woman—but his performance on the rest was very, very poor. Like maybe worthy of an F. How did the guy who'd pulled off a *perfect* engagement mess this up so bad?

I realized Brook was oblivious to the mutually useful items I pack when we go places. The sunscreen, Band-Aids, chargers . . . the things I remember and schlep around that he also uses. That was annoying. But it was also okay. We were partners now, so really only one of us needed to remember the sunscreen. Partnership isn't a perfect division of labor, but ideally it's a union that builds on each other's strengths and makes it easier to get things done. Brook may not notice that I pack ibuprofen, but he appreciates it when he has a headache. I might not realize how much his camera equipment weighs, but I love the organized, color-corrected photos of our trips.

We pulled up to our apartment seventy-two hours later, with greasy hair and unregulated hormones. When my period showed up a week early I had Brook to thank. Good thing he packed all those tampons.

Quiz Time

JILL: Back in Washington, I was sitting at a bar waiting for a friend when a guy came by and looked over my shoulder. "What's that you're studying? Should I get you a drink to help you concentrate?"

"Oh, it's actually a Red Sox study guide," I responded. Then, employing one of the great benefits of engaged life, I casually rested my chin on my left hand, accentuating the ring.

"Oh, cool! I love the Sox. Why are you studying, though?" Damn it, I had assumed the true value of a diamond was that it saved you from talking to people you weren't interested in. This guy needed an f-bomb to get the hint.

"Well, actually my boyfriend, err, fiancé, loves the Sox and he's quizzing me on them later tonight. I'm quizzing him on California." That got rid of him. I was alone with my notes and had two hours until the big test.

I'd been looking forward to this date for a while. There are things that are important to our partners that we don't know much about, and part of being a good spouse is learning to care, at least a little, about those things. Maybe even learn to enjoy them. You don't have to do it for everything; I didn't want to watch Charlie Rose interviews and I doubted Brook would ever appreciate *The Real Housewives*. But I could sit through an occasional *60 Minutes*, and it was obviously no sacrifice for him to watch *Inside Amy Schumer*. Embracing some of each other's interests would make our life together that much easier.

Brook grew up in New England as a huge sports fan, so the Red Sox were like gods to Little Brook. He's described them as the "single most important thing" in his early life, a love that carried into adulthood.

For some women that would be a problem, but I grew up in a sports-focused house as well, playing high school volleyball, basketball, and softball—even boys' Little League for a couple of years. I legitimately liked sports. In our years together, I had seen a ton of Red Sox games but didn't know that much about their "long, proud history." I was actually excited to learn.

I approached this date as I would any quiz, by building a study guide. First stop, the Red Sox Wikipedia page. I jotted down important dates, retired numbers, crucial games. I watched ESPN's documentary on their 2004 American League Championship win and, no joke, it brought tears to my eyes.

I spent far less time building my own quiz for Brook. I didn't have any obvious obsessions, so I kept it simple and chose my home state, California. I wanted him to appreciate where I came from, maybe even learn a little geography. I tried to write questions based on things he might have to know on future trips or that might come up in conversation with my family. *Put these cities in order north to south: L.A., San Diego, Truckee, Palo Alto, Napa, San Francisco* and *Name six of the nine undergrad University of California campuses*. The only rule was that everything on the quiz had to be something the test-giver knew off the top of their head. The winner would get a massage.

When my friend met me at the bar, I asked her to take the California quiz. "Umm, this is way too hard, Jill. He's not going to know this, nor should he have to!" I was a little screwed; we were doing the date in thirty minutes and I couldn't really change it. *Oh well, sorry, Brook.* It looked like I might get that massage. I walked home repeating, "1903, 1912, 1915, 1916, 1918, 2004, 2007, 2013," the eight times the Red Sox had won the World Series. He had to be asking that!

BROOK: We sat at the dining room table and prepared to exchange tests. "I don't want to brag," Jill said, "but I know Ted Williams's nickname." I must have looked impressed, or maybe skeptical.

"Yes, it's the . . . the Stealth Sprinter," she said. I started cracking up.

"I think you mean the Splendid Splinter."

She seemed embarrassed and then confused. "What does that even mean?"

"I don't know, 'splinter' like a piece of the bat, and 'splendid' because he's really good. And they just put it together because of alliteration. I didn't come up with these names."

It can be hard to explain how big sports are in New England unless you've lived there. "We care about sports too," people say everywhere. But sports—and really, mainly the Red Sox—have a special, central place in New England life. In D.C., people talk about politics; in Nashville, they talk about music; in L.A., they talk about themselves. In Boston, it's the Sox.

At some point in the future, Jill would be milling around the grill on a Fourth of July and sprinkling in a "Big Papi" reference wouldn't be good enough anymore. Quinn would know the full batting order and pitching rotation; she'd know whose contract was up at the end of the year. This quiz was a public service, an investment in Jill's acceptance as a Silva-Braga.

We each handed the other our twenty questions and I immediately realized Jill's test on California would be . . . hard. "What is California's largest agricultural export by revenue?" *Wine?* "What is California's state flower?" *Tulip?* Nope and nope.

I had crafted a somewhat easier quiz about the Red Sox and tried to keep it fun. "Question #5: Red Sox great Carl Yastrzemski shared a nickname with this popular birth control pill."

When we tallied our grades I managed only nine out of twenty right. Yikes. Jill aced her test. Seventeen correct! She's a good student, and I appreciated the effort. She was going all-in on joining Team Silva-Braga. It was sweet.

Teach Me What You Do

BROOK: There comes a time when you can no longer ask a question. Like when you've met someone for the fifth time and don't know their name. Can't ask. Something like that had happened between Jill and me. What did she do at work, exactly? It was awkwardly late to ask.

The question came up in conversation pretty often: "What does your girlfriend do?"

"She's basically a business lady," I would say. It was a funny phrase, *business lady.* A lot of our friends had taken to calling Jill a business lady, because it was kind of silly and mainly true and we really had no idea what she did.

She was, I could confidently say, "a senior executive advisor for a leading research and advisory firm that pays for most of our rent, all of our meals, and what meager savings we have left." She went to work around 8 A.M., came home when it was time for dinner, and went on enough business trips that when we needed to rent a car, her Hertz points usually covered it. So what did she do, exactly?

We sat on our couch and opened her laptop. I wanted to understand her work, not only so I could competently answer the question once and for all, but so I could appreciate her successes and challenges, and maybe even help with them.

"So this is my calendar for the week," she started. The screen was filled with orange and gray boxes, external and internal meetings, she explained. *What a clever way to organize your schedule*, I thought. I kept that to myself because I imagined it was standard business lady practice. My calendar was kept mentally, unless I had a lot to remember, in which case I drafted an e-mail to myself listing what I was supposed to do. Hers was a much more *grown-up* way of running a life.

"So let's start here on Monday," she said. "My first meeting was with Joe's Pharmaceutical Company." Actually, the company had a different name, one you would hear if you watched the evening news or an NFL game, but it seems safer not to mention any actual clients. These are the people paying our rent and taking me out to dinner.

"A couple of months ago the CTO at Joe's gave us five areas of their R&D process they were looking to improve on. So for this meeting Monday we presented him with these resources to address each of those areas."

Then she shuttled ahead a couple of days. "Fred's Tractor Company wanted to streamline their R&D process, so I've been working with them," she said. She opened up a PowerPoint document with a thirty-step flowchart crowded onto a single slide. "I'm pretty proud of this because I gave them this piece . . . and this piece." She pointed at a box in the middle of the page and then a circle filled with more text. The details were shrouded in jargon but I actually had a decent sense of what she was doing.

"So your day is kind of split between meeting with your team, talking to these executives about their problems, and then presenting research to them to try to address their problems." She nodded. It was true, she was a business lady, and now I had some idea what that meant.

JILL: You know those old commercials where a dorky-looking fella in a suit (PC) faces off against a cool young guy in a T-shirt and jeans (Mac)? As we reviewed my color-coded calendar I realized that was Brook and me. I worked for "the man" and earned a regular biweekly salary. Brook was his own boss who determined what he wanted to work on and controlled the finished product. I'd been trained to refine processes to make something X percent faster or Y percent cheaper. Brook worked as a creative mind making something new. We existed in different worlds.

Even so, it had always been easy to explain Brook's job: "He makes documentaries" or "He's the guy on the news." And from my non-expert perspective, he seemed to be really good at it, having sold his movies to MTV, National Geographic, and CNBC and reported for the *Washington Post* and CBS. But what always impressed me the most was that his work touched people. He still got notes from strangers saying his documentary *A Map for Saturday* had inspired them to change their lives and travel the world. He brushed that off like it was no big deal, but to me it was so impressive and special.

But *how* did he do his job every day? Best I could tell it was a mixture of finding overlooked stories, maintaining lots of contacts, and mastering complicated electronic equipment. I traveled with him as

he shot one of his documentaries in China, but my contribution to
that project was mainly taking selfies with him in the background
working. For this date, I was going to learn how to actually film.

Brook pulled his newest purchase out of its padded bag and
handed me a Canon video camera shaped like a breadbox. The C100
felt heavy, breakable, and *super*-unwieldy. For one, it was festooned
with buttons, every available space covered with a switch labeled in
jargon—ISO/GAIN, WFM, ZEBRA. It was hard to even hold it
without accidentally pressing one. When I finally found my grip, the
camera was still top-heavy and dense; I couldn't really hold it steady.

"Lesson number one: Use a tripod," Brook started. "You'll see
lots of bozos with no tripod who can't hold the camera steady. Even
with the best camera, their stuff will look awful." I nodded. I'd heard
this speech before. At our friend's recent wedding he had sighed
heavily as the videographer stumbled around. "Would it kill him to
use a tripod?"

"Got it," I said. My arms were already tired anyway.

"Okay, lesson number two: The main thing you have to pay
attention to is the amount of light you're letting into the camera."
He showed me three ways to manage the light.

"All right, now for your test, film me walking around." He theat-
rically opened the fridge and I fiddled with the buttons trying to get
the light right. When I went to hit record he'd already moved to
another part of the room, where it was darker. So I went back to the
buttons and changed the ISO. Hit record. We were rolling!

"Okay, Brook, pretend you're sad." He made a pouty face. "Now,
you just won a million dollars." Excitement. We were laughing, but
then I realized I'd forgotten to focus the damn thing. The shot, while
correctly lit, was unusable. I kept trying for a few more minutes, but
my God, shooting video was *so hard*; you had to manage so many

factors while keeping it steady and focused. And we weren't even dealing with microphones or lights yet! It wasn't until we did this date that I appreciated the years of work Brook put in to learn the skills that most people in his industry outsourced to someone else.

As we put everything away, I asked if we could do it again sometime. "I'd like to learn to shoot better. It'd be cool if I could help you on a future project." He said sure. I pictured that for a moment—Brook and Jill, husband and wife, shooting stories out in the great wide world. It certainly was a different vision than my corporate career path, but one that seemed exciting and actually attainable, though it would take a bunch more work. And much more focus.

DATE #32

Personality Swap

JILL: Rather than continuing to enjoy the blissful high of our engagement, Brook and I soon began the date I'd been dreading since the start of this project. We were swapping personalities for a day, each trying to act like the other, forcing us to see ourselves reflected back through the eyes of our future spouse. "That sounds like a terrible idea," several friends observed.

I was already in a grumpy mood when I came home from a stressful day of work and greeted myself. Well, I greeted Brook as me, greeting me as Brook. (S)he was bouncing off the walls with energy, running around the room and talking nonstop before I even took my shoes off.

"So we're already starting?" I sighed, dropping my computer bag by the door. I had little hope of achieving relationship enlightenment in the next few hours; my goal was basically survival. In a bid to be a good sport, I promptly "lost" my phone and when *Jill* found it for me I buried my head in the screen and tweeted, *Observation about football based on my sports TV background*. Get it? Brook's bad at keeping track of his things and tweets a lot about sports.

But despite this heroic attempt to overcome my bad mood, the date was not going well. I didn't want Brook making fun of me and I didn't like making fun of him. And anyway I only had two ideas left—(1) Go to the bathroom for twenty minutes before bed, and (2) fix the TV.

Brook was giving it his best Daniel Day-Lewis–style effort. He came out of the shower with a towel covering his chest and another wrapped around his head. "Uggg, my boobs hurt," he complained before dropping the lower towel and chugging water in the buff. I laughed and tried to take a deep breath.

Brook's rendition of *Jill* was good enough to make me appreciate how intense my energy and talkativeness could be. Yes, *Jill* was funny, but she also required a lot of attention and failed to pick up on some not-so-subtle clues that *Brook* needed a few quiet moments. That tension would probably always exist, but we had proven by now it wouldn't be fatal.

I used to think "partnership" was finding someone with similar life goals who would celebrate your successes and comfort you during your worst moments. That was certainly part of it. But as I matured, and especially as I went through these dates, I came to understand that no matter who we end up with they're going to be a hot mess in some way. Brook knew I could get in a bad mood at the drop of a hat, but he learned how to handle those fifteen painful minutes before I calmed down. I knew Brook would lose his keys under the same seat cushion at least once a week for the next twenty years, and I didn't really care. The magic of partnership is finding someone who can love you in spite of yourself, someone willing to adapt to your personality quirks and vice versa. Brook and I somehow managed to put up with each other like no one else could.

But then . . . oh sweet Brook, why did you do this . . . he decided it was time for some fitness. He dramatically changed into workout clothes, went to the living room, did one push-up, and stormed back to me. "I'm *so* bad at working out, I just hate it." I started crying almost instantly. Crying was one thing the real Jill could definitely do more believably than the pretend *Jill*.

BROOK: To play Jill I needed bursts of kinetic energy that came unnaturally to me. For weeks I tried to build lists of things to talk about, so I could simulate her encyclopedia of conversation starters. Even with prep time I failed. So I just ran around the house doing and saying a lot of stuff and that quickly rubbed her the wrong way. We could trade personalities but that didn't change who we were—Jill was more sensitive than me. I probably should have known better.

But I felt okay joking about these things because they didn't seem to matter so much anymore. The constant talking, the whining about working out . . . yeah, they might still be issues in the future but they were issues I believed we had worked through enough to laugh about. If I'd made an FYI List, they'd no longer be on it. After I saw her tears I tried to make that clearer to Jill, that I could love her unconditionally without every aspect of her personality being my absolute preference. Maybe Jill had to reach that understanding herself. But I could do my part to help.

"Okay, executive fiancé decision here," I said. "Worrying about working out is coming off your FYI List. I'm doing it for you, it's off, the list is empty, there is no list!"

Maybe I was getting overconfident, but in the last couple of weeks I'd felt we made real progress toward building a house we'd be comfortable in for a long time: Appreciating each other's work, studying up on important parts of our past, even learning where she keeps her tampons (*I'm kidding, Jill*) were all bricks we were stacking together. And I *did* appreciate that Jill packed the phone chargers and sunscreen (*I'm serious, Jill*) and I hoped she appreciated that I did the laundry and made the TV work. The beauty of the thing was that I would never have to remember the sunscreen again, and she would never have to learn how the TV was wired. Partnership was the great efficiency of truly being a couple.

Marriage Prep

DATE #33 (PART ONE)

How Will We Say "I Do"?

JILL: "Do you mind if I offer some unsolicited advice?" he asked. Maurice, a married coworker and father of five-year-old twins had an engagement recommendation for me. This was back on the Monday after Brook got down on one knee and I'd just spilled the big news, which basically involved walking around the office until people noticed the ring. Maurice offered some sweet congratulations and then launched into his pitch.

"Don't start planning your wedding yet. Just take a while and enjoy being engaged. It's a special time you'll never get back, and once you start planning the wedding it disappears."

He was right, but we didn't listen.

I blame everyone else. *When are you getting married?* I still had a champagne hangover when they started asking. At first it was novel and cute: "Oh we don't know yet! This is all just so new and exciting!" Then, the question started to make me feel like we were behind schedule, "I'm not sure, but we only got engaged last weekend." Finally, it was just confusing. Did these people—many of them only acquaintances—actually *care* about my wedding? Could they really not find anything else to ask?

There were probably plenty of brides who yearned to talk about their wedding; in fact, my Facebook feed was cluttered by them. That just wasn't me. It was strange really. Getting engaged was the single most exciting thing that had ever happened to me, and it felt so wonderful sharing that joy with friends and family. But talking about *weddings* just wasn't as fun. Part of me blamed the summers I spent catering in high school and college, rocking a tuxedo shirt and bow tie, serving grilled shrimp and wedding cake.

That was when I learned weddings turn perfectly rational people into monsters. There was one bride who kept her guests waiting two hours in the summer heat so she could finish her makeup; we ran out of shrimp. Another kept referring to the staff as "my people," ordering us around just because she could. Those were the clear bridezillas, and luckily they weren't all that common. But more often, seemingly nice people became super stressed and struggled to enjoy their "perfect day." I could understand that stress; I'd seen the invoices and knew how much money it took to throw a pretty average reception.

So it should have been easy to take Maurice's advice, especially since Brook and I thought we already knew what kind of wedding we wanted. Months before, we had skipped ahead to this date, caught up in a romantic, slightly boozy dinner at a nice French restaurant. "I know we aren't supposed to do this date until later," Brook said, "but what if we just did a thought experiment about what our hypothetical wedding might look like." So we started fantasizing, sharing for the first time our visions for a wedding day.

BROOK: We turned on the tape recorder just as a carafe of wine arrived. Listening to that chat now, it is overwhelmingly quaint, like reading your elementary school essay on career plans after you've retired. "Hi, future Brook and Jill," she laughed into the recorder. "Hope everything is going great."

Right away, we agreed we didn't love the idea of a traditional wedding. "I really don't want to plan a wedding," Jill said. "I don't want to spend a year of my life talking to you about RSVPs and getting people's addresses and you having to remember to buy the cuff links as a groom's present." I agreed and suggested we could just rent a big house somewhere in the Caribbean and invite a couple dozen friends and family to spend a wedding week with us.

I always found wedding receptions vaguely tragic—you spent so many hours and so many dollars throwing a party for everyone you knew and then, because it was so brief and because there were so many people, you hardly spent time with anyone. A friend might travel two thousand miles across the country to visit for the first time in years and you would spend three or four minutes with him. It was like a nightmare—not a metaphor for something bad, but an actual bad dream—in which all the people closest to you were within reach but you couldn't talk to them.

We wanted to avoid that five-hour, debt-inducing reception. So I liked this idea of replacing a wedding day with a wedding week and inviting only a handful of people who were profoundly important to us, important enough that they'd want to spend a week with us. With the money we'd save by not having a traditional reception, we could rent a big house for our friends. It was an exciting idea, and it fit our style as a couple, but it created a huge problem: By keeping the group so small, we wouldn't be able to invite most of our friends and family. So maybe something bigger and more inclusive was the better option . . . but that just led us back in the direction of the traditional wedding we said we didn't want.

"This is hard," Jill said as she emptied the carafe of wine. "This is why people end up having a big wedding. It's the easiest option." But the couple talking on the tape were cute. They were excited and optimistic and naïve. They would come to learn that planning a wedding wasn't as simple as renting a house for twenty-five of your friends, but at the time they were just jazzed by the thought of it.

"I hope I get to plan a wedding with you someday," Jill said. "If you play your cards right."

"Maybe you'll finally ask me," I joked.

"Oh man, you'd be so mad if I asked you to marry me."

"That's true." It was nice to listen to the tape and know it hadn't come to that. There would be real wedding planning, just not quite yet.

DATE #34

Take My Name

BROOK: First we had to deal with some nitty-gritty. Before we could get married there were decisions to make. Like what we'd call ourselves. I logged out of my Gmail account and signed up for a new one, BrookAndres79@gmail.com. For a week I would take Jill's name and she'd take mine, test-driving new titles before any legal name change that might come with marriage. I pulled up my Twitter profile and became Brook Andres. Man, that looked funny.

This struck a deep vein in me. My name has been a source of constant minor irritation my entire life. First off, there's "Brook," a name chosen because it was supposedly unisex, though after thirty years of research I can confidently estimate 99 percent of us Brooks are women. It's an ongoing annoyance, like when a pharmacist wants to know my relation to the woman whose prescription I'm picking up.

But my last name was worse. I was christened Brook Silva but since kindergarten had gone by Brook Silva-Braga. The hyphen is a special kind of curse, a constant extra barrier to communicating who you are.

"Silva-Braga. No, Silva isn't the first name, it's all one last name. Silva, S-I-L-V-A and then hyphen, like a dash, Braga, B-R-A-G-A ... No, none of it is a middle name, it's all one name. Yes, it's a capital B. No, my mom kept her name, she's Silva, my dad's Braga." And worst of all, the hyphen solved nothing. It passed the problem to me and my eventual wife. Were Jill and I supposed to become Mr. and Mrs. Andres-Silva-Braga? Lord no! Choices had to be made.

I logged into my new Gmail account and Brook Andres started to write to a former coworker. But I wasn't sure how to start; I felt a need to identify myself, to explain. For a moment I wondered if the message could just wait until next week. Our names are our identity, especially online, where we aren't recognized by our voice or face. Mine was suddenly gone; I had to reintroduce myself to my best friends.

But the reality was, at least one of us would have to face this annoyance, unless we both just kept our names like my parents had and created some new kind of headache for our children. Becoming Brook Andres gave me a much deeper appreciation for all the women who had changed their names for their husbands; it was a real sacrifice. Yes, it was a tradition from a time of less gender equality, but it remained the best option I could see. My parents' generation had tried to throw off those shackles but gave their kids a new kind of problem.

What's in a name? William Shakespeare asked. Brook Silva-Braga answers: The potential for a lifetime of hassle. And you should have known that, William; there are six surviving signatures of your name and in each one you spelled it differently.

So who was Brook Andres? I didn't recognize him. Being the guy with the funny name had always been this little barrier to communicating who I was, but it also came with the benefit of having a name people remembered. I sat there at my computer with my new name and it freaked me out. I didn't want to change.

JILL: Brook and I were slurping the last of our phở when the dinner bill arrived. "I'll get this one," I offered, and put down my credit card. But when the receipt came back I paused at the sight of the blank line at the bottom of the slip. This was the first time signing my new name, Gillian Silva-Braga. I put pen to paper, squiggled a "G," worked my way through "Silva," forgot the hyphen and struggled to even finish "Braga." My cursive had never been good, but my God, this name was hard to sign! I filled the back of the receipt with failed attempts.

I appreciated how seriously Brook took the date. He changed his name quite publicly on Twitter and started e-mailing my family under his new alias, including one group chain I was on that ended with his reply-all, "I'm not sure Jill Silva-Braga should be on this Andres-only e-mail."

But let's be honest, this date was really more about me and whether I was willing to change my name. It was a decision nearly every married woman, but only a few men, were forced to make. One survey I read found that most Americans don't believe men should even be *allowed* to take their wife's name!

I'd seen my girlfriends try out every imperfect option. Meghan Bell kept her name; we had always called her "Bell" and still could. But most friends followed tradition and changed their names, at least partially. It was a tough personal choice for most women, but for ladies with strong professional brands it was even tougher. Some of my journalist friends changed their names legally but kept their old bylines.

Whatever your choice, someone wouldn't like it. One lawyer friend took her husband's name and came back from their honeymoon to find a demoralizing e-mail from a female colleague: "Congrats on your marriage. I was surprised to see your new e-mail address; most professional women don't change their name." *Thanks*.

For ladies who kept their names, it got trickier when babies joined the mix. Most opted to give their kids Dad's name, leaving the woman to either finally, begrudgingly change or be left with a different name than her kids. A few girlfriends who stuck with their maiden names developed creative aliases for their brood. Baby Jack's parents, Jen Yost and Jack Swetland, informally called themselves the Swosts. It was a cute workaround, but the birth certificate didn't say Jack Swost. "Actually, some of us want that as a real name not a funny joke," Jen said when I asked her about it.

I'd always had a very strong and unwavering expectation that my husband, my children, and I would all have the same name. I wasn't typically a traditionalist, but I felt society had a point on this one. Names are how families identify themselves. If I was going to build a family, I wanted to sound like a family. I assumed that meant I'd change my name one day; after all, that's how it's normally done and I was the one who felt strongly about having the same name.

But now that I was engaged, the clock was running out on Jill

Andres. All of a sudden changing my name felt like a big sacrifice, a life-defining decision. It was the little things that triggered that feeling, like an e-mail from my mom: "Okay, tickets to Raychel's wedding are booked, all the Andres will be there!" My excitement gave way to unexpected grief. Obviously I'd still be an Andres if I became a Silva-Braga, but . . . actually I wouldn't be. I'd be different than my brother and sister, my parents, even my nieces.

My monogramed GVA necklace caught my eye a lot more that week. My mom had given it to me years before and I never took it off. Would I keep wearing it if the initials were wrong? I'd be giving up a lot of the things I loved about who I was to become a Silva-Braga.

Did you know many U.S. counties require women to decide their married names before they can get a marriage license? Many of my friends were unaware of this, and were caught off guard when they had to make their name decision on the spot. (It struck me as strange, though, that they hadn't decided sooner. How did your family's future name not come up in all those months you were deciding on tablecloth fabric and stamp design? Probably because it was a discussion many preferred to avoid.) I wasn't interested in postponing this decision until the last minute, so Brook and I sat down at the end of the week to settle our name plan.

Brook went first. "I think this date really forced me to recognize the sacrifice and inconvenience of changing your name. I'm not more willing to change mine, but I have an increased understanding if you don't want to change yours." He'd gotten the point; the date had worked.

My turn. "It felt fun to try out this new identity and to feel closer to your family. The fact is, and I'm going to be transparent, I want my family to all have the same name. If that means me changing my name, I'm willing to do that, though obviously it's a big sacrifice."

"What if we all had the same name, but I went by a different name professionally?" Brook suggested. He was offering alternatives to taking his complex handle, but I didn't bite. Our name situation was already complicated enough; I wanted to end up with one name we'd all use all the time. No half-steps here. I suddenly, and sort of embarrassingly, realized we'd skipped over something important.

"You know, I've assumed that you'd want me to take your name," I said. "But you've never asked." Brook's parents had been married thirty-two years and never shared a last name; maybe he didn't expect that we would either.

He smiled and grabbed my hand. "I would be flattered if you changed your name." He paused and continued, "But if you change yours I'll have to change mine too."

"Change your name to what?" I was confused. And then I remembered that he had gone by Brook Silva-Braga since kindergarten but was still legally Brook Silva. "Yeah, I can't be taking this name if it's not even your real one!" And so we'd reached a decision—both of us would legally change our name to Silva-Braga. Rather than sad or scared, I felt settled. Excited even. We were really doing this. We were actually going to be a family soon.

DATE #35

Downer Docs

JILL: An e-mail popped into my work inbox a few days later. "Please review and update your emergency contact information ASAP." I looked at the note and noticed that my parents, who lived three thousand miles away, were still listed. For the first time in my thirty-two years, I had an update. Brook would be my new emergency contact. That night I told him about his new obligations should my plane crash or appendix burst, and that got us thinking about all the sad things we might face as husband and wife—the "in sickness" part of our upcoming vows.

This was the start of our heaviest date yet, "Downer Docs," where we would get into the details of things we'd rather not think about—living wills, family support, even a possible prenuptial agreement.

Everyone loves talking about the wonderful, exciting parts of joining your lives, but the reality is there are also hard, sad responsibilities you take on when you get married. Brook and I were now in a position to make life-or-death decisions for each other, and we took the job seriously.

"Okay, so let's imagine that you've been in a car accident and you're in a coma," I started. The image of him bruised and broken in a hospital hooked up to a bunch of machines flashed through my head. It was enough to get the waterworks going. "At what percent likelihood that you'll never recover should I decide to stop treatment?" It was such a weird concept, I struggled to even piece together a coherent question.

"Do you mean fully recover or survive?" he asked.

"Umm, I don't really know what I mean, actually." This stuff was so nebulous and emotional.

"Well, I'd say that if they tell you I have a one percent chance of recovery in the next year you should keep giving me treatment."

"What if they say you'll survive but be brain dead?"

He had to think about that one. "Then you should probably pull the plug."

We went back and forth for a while throwing out nightmare scenarios, giving each other guidance about when we'd want to fight and when we thought injuries were too brutal to overcome.

We couldn't possibly outline all the potential scenarios, but the conversation made one thing clear: Brook had more will to live than

I did. I instructed him to pull the plug earlier in almost every situation. That insight was extremely valuable. I think it's natural to assume our partners view things the same way we do, so without this conversation I would have probably been a little too willing to "let nature run its course" for Brook. If I'm ever in the situation to have to make these types of decisions they'll obviously be heart-wrenching, but I'd feel at least some solace knowing that I was carrying out his wishes, and vice versa. But, my lord, I hope it never comes to that.

BROOK: There was a heavy cloud over us by the end of the living will chat. When I looked across the plaza where we were sitting I saw rows of hospital beds with Jill and me lying in them, unresponsive. We got up and strolled a couple of blocks, trying to walk away from that feeling. We decided to wait until the next morning to finish the date.

When I was just out of college in my first adult job, a bunch of older coworkers started planning weddings. They were mainly excited about getting married. But I have a distinct memory of sharing lunch with two of them and asking what a soon-to-be-married couple did about a prenuptial agreement.

"What do you do?" they answered rhetorically. "You don't ever bring it up! They'll kill you for even mentioning a prenup. It is not an option."

Jill was more reasonable than that; she'd already agreed to discuss it as part of this date. But the next morning the emotional sky was still gray. Over lunch, we started to talk through different prenup scenarios to understand how divorce would impact the financial situation of each case.

From the start Jill was aggressively critical of whatever I said, taking a defensive tone I recognized from other tough conversations. I was trying to discuss this in a rational, dispassionate way. I was

good (probably too good) at separating my thoughts from my feelings, so I was discussing the mechanics of a prenup separately from
the emotional meaning of a prenup. "If we got divorced and you had
made a lot of money, you'd be protected from me taking half of it," I
said. Jill sat there icily, for once playing the role of the silent partner.

I was expressing my *thoughts* about prenups. My *feelings* about
them were more complicated. In an era when divorce has very little
social cost, the financial burden of separation almost seemed like a
good thing. Getting out of a marriage *should* be hard; do we really
need a contract to make it easier? But I didn't come out and say all
that right away, I played it a bit coy to gauge Jill's honest response,
bringing up scenarios where I thought a prenup made sense, testing
what her reaction would be if I did want one. It did not seem positive.

But even the legal aspects of a prenup were hard to discuss
because divorce law varies so much by state (and country). A good
general baseline is this: The money you have before you're married
remains yours after divorce, but whatever you make or combine
while you're married is split 50/50 after divorce. There are endless
exceptions to that simplification.

Still, to the extent that simplification was true, it meant a prenup
didn't make much sense for Jill and me. I had some savings, she had
some college debt, but the amounts weren't that big. Plus, we had similar earning potential—it was unlikely one of us would make millions
and then lose half if we got divorced. And even if that happened, the
other partner would arguably deserve it since their support and sacrifice would have helped make it possible.

So as a theoretical concept I was conflicted about prenups, and in
practice they didn't seem to matter much to us. But I could imagine it
making sense for other couples. (Some years before, I dated a woman
from a very rich family and I think if I married her I would have pre-

ferred some kind of prenup just to make clear that I wasn't marrying her family's money.)

"For us, I don't think it makes much sense," I finally said. "I don't want one." This didn't do all that much to improve the mood of the conversation, but it was good to be done with it. There was also probably a lesson for me in being a bit too businesslike when discussing things that Jill would naturally feel emotional about—but that required overcoming my habit of putting feelings off to the side in a little box. I still had generous room for personal improvement.

Jill picked over the lunch she had barely touched. We had one more Downer Doc to pen, and it was the one that worried me the most: whom in our families would we support financially. I had always felt strongly about helping my sister if she ever needed it, and one concern I had about marriage was the limits it would put on me to do that—I might be willing to bankrupt myself for her, but would I lose that option once I was married? And on the other hand, what if Jill wanted to fork over our savings to every distant cousin or college friend who came asking?

We each made a list of loved ones we'd want to support and thankfully they looked quite similar. Then we got an afternoon drink. We had earned it. It had been one of those rare conversations that made us feel awful even as we were very glad to have had it.

DATE #36

House Hunting

BROOK: Our marriage would begin at a ceremony we still needed to plan and probably end in a hospital room we'd always dread, but most of the time in the middle would be spent in our home. What did we want that home to look like? We found a seat at Peregrine Espresso and spread open the classified section of a real, live, physical *Washington Post*. We were going house hunting.

We didn't actually want to buy a house yet; we hoped to live internationally for a couple of years and only settle in as homeowners when we had school-aged kids. In a way that made the exercise more important to do now, because we risked spending the next several years imagining different dream homes. And it turned out that was exactly what we were doing.

"I think over the next ten years I'll want to live in an urban setting," Jill said.

"I'm less hung up on that," I said. "If it's within our means that would be great, but I think there's a reason so many people go to the suburbs." Then I dug into the classifieds. One column listed homes in the District of Columbia, another had houses in suburban Virginia, and a third gave listings for the suburbs of Maryland.

"You already want to jump in and look at stuff," she said sharply.

It turned out we had a fundamental difference of belief: Jill wanted to live in the city and thought people who moved to the suburbs went because they wanted that lifestyle; I also preferred staying in the city but thought new parents ended up in the 'burbs because it turned out to be much cheaper and easier and we might end up reaching the same conclusion. I also feared that most of what we liked about the city—walkable restaurants, bars, and theaters—wouldn't be as important when we had kids. Jill was still holding on to the dream she nursed the day we borrowed Jack, that she could roll a stroller to a café like the one we were sitting in. I didn't mention that we had rolled right past this café the day we borrowed Jack.

We reached a working compromise: If we both still felt this way when it came time to buy, I'd be willing to turn my soft preference for the city into an official plan to stay there since it was Jill's strong preference. So we limited our search to the D.C. city limits and found an open house about a mile away. We walked up Fourteenth Street to the outskirts of Columbia Heights and found four newly built units in a refurbished three-story building. It was a quiet block of an increasingly upscale neighborhood and when we reached the freshly painted building there was a hand-scrawled sign tied to the neighbor's porch: "Ugly popups ruin neighborhood diversity."

We had met the gentrifiers, and we were them.

JILL: Brook and I moseyed into a paint-scented apartment and were quickly spotted by the real estate agent. "Hello, thanks for coming." His voice echoed around the empty, white-walled living room. I was certain he could tell we didn't belong, like a couple of sixteen-year-olds trying to blend in at an R-rated movie. We hadn't bothered to put together a believable backstory beyond "We're just starting to look." What happened if he started asking questions about . . . about anything, really?

Another couple came in behind us and a third was milling in the kitchen. All of us were thirty-something professionals. Brook and I actually fit in perfectly.

As we walked through the apartment, every room seemed to prompt a conversation we had prepared for by doing the forty dates, like the too-perfect end of a *Karate Kid* movie where all of Mr. Miyagi's training techniques resurface as the solutions to Daniel-san's problems. Thanks to our *Money* dates, we knew which of the four units were in our price range. The *Kids* dates established our family plans, and Brook walked into a small bedroom wondering whether the baby would sleep there or if we'd use the bigger bedroom as a nursery and play space.

"Huh, there are two bathrooms on this level; we could each have our own," Brook noted, implying that some of our "It's a Chore" issues might be defused by a spacious layout. It was a conversation we couldn't possibly have had thirty-six dates earlier.

Everything in the apartment was brand new and low quality, so we wondered if we'd rather handle renovations ourselves. But would we really want to renovate a house while raising small kids and moving to a new city? There were so many considerations we'd never imagined. This wasn't going to be our actual home, we weren't ready to buy, but like any good training sequence it prepared us for the real thing. We had a lot to figure out about our life before we'd be ready to settle down and buy a place, but even with all that uncertainty there was so much we did know. At the very least, when I closed my eyes and pictured my future home, I knew who would be there with me. We could pick out paints and bedroom sets later. First, we had to make this whole thing official. We needed to plan a wedding.

DATE #33 (PART TWO)

How Will We Say "I Do"?

BROOK: We sat at our computer looking at the Casa Capitan availability calendar and picked the second week of November for our wedding. It was only a few months away, which would make for a short engagement, which was exactly what we wanted—less time to agonize over the details. And amazingly we had decided to do almost exactly what we had fantasized about over that French dinner many months before: We were renting a big house on the beach in Santa Teresa, Costa Rica, and filling it with twenty-four of our closest friends and family.

Even using the spare emergency bunk bed in a windowless room, twenty-four guests were all that would fit. Each of us could invite just twelve people. So Jill began listing the folks she absolutely needed to invite, and then she would see what space was left for everyone else. When she finished her must-come list she counted the names. Thirty-five. Oh no.

Jill seemed right on the edge of scrapping Costa Rica. Twelve people? She couldn't make a list of just twelve people! Five of her spots were taken by her immediate family, so that really only left her seven invites. What about her best friend from college? What about her aunt and cousins? How were they all supposed to fit? "You have a smaller family," she said. But really she meant, *You're willing to leave your aunts and cousins behind and I'm not.*

And that was how we ended up planning three weddings. We had wanted to avoid a traditional wedding and instead ended up with three: My parents and I would have a reception in Rhode Island for family and friends on the East Coast, Jill and her family would have one in California for folks on the West Coast, and we would hold the actual ceremony in Costa Rica.

But even three weddings didn't appease everyone. One weekend that summer we crashed up in New York with our friend Jaimie, the twenty-fifth person on the Casa Capitan guest list. We figured someone would say they couldn't come to Costa Rica and we'd sneak her in, but it was looking like all twenty-four would say yes. Jaimie was a really close friend—she was with us on the raft in Uganda that day Jill lost her tooth; she'd spent a month traveling across India with Jill; she'd helped get my first documentary on MTV, giving me a career in filmmaking.

The three of us woke up in Jaimie's apartment on a Saturday morning and Jill mentioned that she was disappointed Jaimie wouldn't be able to come to Costa Rica. It was news to Jaimie. So when Jill went off to brunch with some other friends, Jaimie and I took a walk on the path along the Hudson River and I tried to explain how it had come to this.

"You really want to have a wedding that your friends can't come to?" Jaimie asked.

"Yeah, it's really tough, but it's going to give our families a chance to spend a lot of time together and we just didn't want to do the big five-hour reception where we don't really get to spend time with anyone."

Jaimie did not look even a little bit convinced. "How are Jason and Deb dealing with not getting to come?" she asked. I stopped walking and reached out to give Jaimie a hug.

"I'm so sorry. But they are coming." Jaimie was quiet for a long while. We invited her to the party in Rhode Island and the party in California, but she said she couldn't make it to either.

JILL: So Brook and Jill, two low-key, nontraditional people, were planning not one, not two, but three weddings. We thought we were better than this! But no, the moment you start organizing *your own* wedding, all the things you've always thought about *everyone else's* wedding go out the window. Somehow the emotional power of planning this event with so much symbolic significance overcomes your ability to see the world as it is. When you're wearing the bridesmaid's dress it's obvious how ugly and overpriced it is, but that same dress at your own wedding is a trendy bargain. "The girls will definitely be able to reuse it, fuchsia is really *in* right now."

I wouldn't do that! I would have just one bridesmaid (my sister) and she could choose her own damn dress. But while I was busy avoiding one wedding trap, I fell into others.

Ironically, once we survived the very awkward process of figuring out the Costa Rica guest list, our actual wedding was the easiest of the three to plan. It involved fun tasks like booking ziplining, chartering a fishing trip, and organizing surfing lessons. I found a Badgley Mischka wedding dress online for $169 and it fit perfectly. Our friend Katie, the girl who introduced us all those years before in Boston, would perform the ceremony. It would be lovely but it came at the cost of planning these two other parties. And that was my fault. "I always thought if we were going to do a destination wedding then I would also want to have receptions back home for each of us," I'd said during the wedding chat at the French restaurant. At the time, I pictured parties at our parents' houses with booze, music, and some simple food. What I didn't appreciate was that there was no simple way to throw a party with your parents for one hundred people. They never had a chance to be humble affairs; they were going to be "wedding receptions" whether we wanted them to be or not. The first law of matrimonial dynamics is that your parents do not help throw you a wedding, they help throw themselves a wedding. I wish I could go back in time and warn myself that even with the best intentions there was no way we could pull off what we originally envisioned.

Suddenly, Brook and I were doing all the things we didn't want to do: approving invitations, debating caterers, picking venues. We had the added treat of negotiating each of these details twice with each set of in-laws. Do you want gold decorations or silver? Do you want a band or a DJ? We wanted none of these things, but we were mainly helpless to stop them.

Brook valiantly fought his parents on every budget-expanding detail, a hopeless effort. By the time we started planning the California party with my family, I was so exhausted and overworked (organizing three weddings, working full time, writing a book, and trying to have a life is a lot to balance!) that I defaulted to my nonconfrontational approach and just avoided making any decisions. That lightened our workload but left us with little input.

It became the first real test of our merged families. It was hard to push back without sounding ungrateful, but it was stressful to stand by and watch our parents spend time and money on things that we considered unnecessary. Wedding planning was a crucible for almost every couple I know, and I could never quite tell if it was a strengthening exercise that prepared them for future challenges or an unnecessary-conflict machine that weakened couples right at the start of their married lives. I did see one upside to the irrational amount of energy we spent on a ceremony that would last just a few minutes—when all those months of preparation culminated in that brief moment, a good part of its power came from the weight of all the effort we'd put into shaping it.

On my orange and gray work calendar I blocked the dates for "Wedding 1 of 3," "Wedding 2 of 3" and "Wedding 3 of 3." They would all be wonderful and lovely, even if it was so much more than we'd intended. When a coworker got engaged a couple of months after me and mentioned a "low-key wedding," I tried to let my experience serve as a cautionary tale. But honestly, when I compared our experience planning our events to some of my friends', I thought we managed pretty well. We had started with a simple, beautiful idea for how we wanted to join our lives and even when reality made that difficult, we had worked together to keep it alive.

The Long Haul

Facing Our Fears

BROOK: In the quiet months before the wedding we booked an impossibly cheap flight to Cancun on the premise that we could take a bus away from the flocks of tourists. But now that we were in Cozumel, that wasn't quite working out. Funny hats and sunburns spilled from the ferry. Souvenirs and frozen drinks lined the water. But Playa del Gringo wasn't all bad: There was perfect weather, a beautiful beach, and the chance to please Jill by going scuba diving. It was one of her great loves and one of my great fears.

On a family vacation the week before starting college I nearly drowned snorkeling. My mask broke in shallow water and I stood up in a bed of sea urchins. With each desperate step their needles filled my feet with unbearable pain; it got so bad that I couldn't use my legs to kick. I held my mask with one hand, leaving me just one arm to paddle. The sixty feet to shore felt like a mile. I made it out of the water but spent the first weeks of college limping on swollen feet. And I developed a dim view of snorkeling.

Jill, meanwhile, spent her college years attached to a scuba tank and it remained one of her favorite hobbies. On past beach vacations, when she signed up to dive I sat on shore and read a book. Going that far underwater just seemed . . . unnatural. But as the years passed, it also seemed wrong to skip out on one of her passions. So when we each decided to conquer a fear, I chose to finally go under.

I signed up for a scuba crash course that, in the lightly regulated world of Mexican diving, soon allowed Jill and me to ride a bouncing speedboat to my first real dive. The main requirement for getting on the boat had been signing my name: "I (participant name), _____, hereby affirm that I am aware that skin and scuba diving have inherent risks which may result in serious injury or death."

I struggled to put on my fins and wet suit as the boat tossed us around. Jill helped strap the heavy oxygen tank to my back. "Okay, now jump in," the captain said impatiently, and I held my mask and fell backward into the Gulf of Mexico.

We were a long way from shore, and the first breaths through the regulator felt very strange. I couldn't seem to breathe in or out quite deeply enough even though the regulator shoved a full gulp of oxygen into my lungs as soon as I took the smallest sip. *People aren't supposed to be down here*, I kept thinking. I would have said it out loud but I couldn't speak. Communication was limited to these dopey "Okay" signs we kept flashing back and forth.

Jill hardly looked at the fish; she mainly focused on staying by my side, closer than the instructor. The dive master after all was protected by rather ironclad legal terms. "I understand and agree that neither the dive professionals conducting this program, nor

PADI Americas, Inc., . . . may be held liable or responsible in any way for any injury, death, or other damages to me." *But he knows I can't tip him if I'm dead*, I reassured myself.

The three of us started sinking farther down, pausing every five or ten feet to clear the pressure from our ears. We reached the bottom and knelt in the sand; for the first time I looked up and saw the glowing blue surface far above us. It was surreal—snorkeling gives the sensation of looking into a room from the ceiling, but this felt like kneeling at the altar of Notre Dame Cathedral. A giant turtle was eating coral nearby and as we approached he flapped gently upward, rising thirty feet until he touched the surface and took a breath. I had already legally affirmed that "Scuba diving is an exciting and demanding activity," but now I felt a more voluntary appreciation.

I was actually glad to be down there with Jill. I couldn't tell her that, but I flashed some "Okay" signs and she flashed them back until I finally noticed how long I'd spent down there not being afraid.

JILL: The inside of the plane was roughly the size of a sports car, only imagine one where all comforts have been stripped out, leaving nothing but a dirty aluminum floor and vibrating walls. I was crammed in there with the pilot, my tandem-skydiving partner, and a barefoot guy with a GoPro strapped to his head. The plane was too small for Brook to fit, so he'd have to be satisfied by watching video of my jump. We were bumpily climbing ten thousand feet above the same water Brook and I had just explored behind scuba masks. To say I was nervous would be a dramatic understatement. In the twenty years my instructor had been making jumps, he said, he could count on one hand the number of clients who looked as frightened as I did.

I know that Brook had a real fear of scuba diving, and to see him overcome that and explore the world in a new way—with me by his side—had been such a rush. Yes, scuba diving could be dangerous. I'd been a hundred feet under when strong currents or too much nitrogen in the brain made it hard to move or make decisions. And Brook's brief training certainly hadn't prepared him for every possibility. But diving in shallow tropical waters like Cozumel's was pretty damn safe. Skydiving . . . well . . . skydiving was never safe. (The skydiving release form made Brook's scuba agreement look like a "No Running Near the Pool" sign). Why would a mentally competent person *pay* for the privilege of throwing herself out of a *perfectly good*—although admittedly uncomfortable—plane?!

I'd always had what I considered a "healthy fear" of heights. I didn't mind climbing a ladder or boarding a plane, but I did get a little wobbly gazing past my toes on the Grand Canyon's glass viewing deck. I'd never even considered skydiving until we created this date and Brook nominated jumping. I accepted the challenge but, as the moment grew nearer, I rapidly lost my nerve. On the sleepless night before our rendezvous with skydiving destiny, my chest became so tight I feared my breaths would stop if I let myself doze off.

The next morning we walked to the skydiving center and discovered that it shared a wall with Señor Frog's, home of yard-tall margaritas and wet T-shirt contests. Just beyond the range of spring breakers' projectile vomit, we found the skydiving staff detangling and repacking used parachutes in a dark hallway, a process that required a shocking amount of parachute kicking and cigarette smoking. By the time we made it into the shop to meet the instructor, I was physically shaking and unsure if I had wet my pants.

After a mere ten minutes of distracted instruction on how to arch your back and step out of the plane, we were already suiting up. I tried to look stoic, but the instructor's expression suggested I might not be succeeding. It all happened so fast. Before I could even kiss Brook good-bye, I'd been whisked to the local airport and ushered to the tiny sports-car-sized aluminum death trap.

I looked less *Top Gun* and more "Baby with Full Diaper." But this wasn't a fashion contest, I reminded myself. I tried to focus on how tight the straps felt (I figured the tighter the better) and when I was supposed to start arching my back.

The air got cold as the plane climbed, or maybe I had shivered myself into a fever. Shaking gave way to full-on tremors. When my tandem partner motioned for me to crawl over to him, I could barely move. But he got us strapped together, both facing forward with him behind me. I realized this was the closest I'd been to another man since Brook and I got back together. And then the door opened and I completely lost it.

What sprung forth were not roller-coaster *This is scary* screams, but uncontrollable *Don't pull the trigger!* shrieks. I tried to remember my "training" and started to slide my foot out onto a ledge half the width of a balance beam while screaming bloody murder. Between the 100-mph wind and my tremors it was hard to get my foot to stick. It slipped the first time, and then again. Finally, and with *a lot* of "help" from my tandem partner, we were out on the ledge, he counted nearly to three, and we tumbled toward the Yucatan.

I almost immediately realized what was happening and must admit it was pretty amazing. We floated below the clouds toward a stunning blue-green carpet. After thirty seconds of freefall, my partner pulled the rip cord and we jolted to a stop. For some, those next ten minutes drifting to Earth would have been exhilarating, but I couldn't stop thinking that our recently kicked parachute could tear at any moment.

When my feet finally touched the sand, it was the first time in days I could take a full breath. But rather than being energized, I felt instantly exhausted. Brook came running down the beach and hugged me, asking how it was. He was so excited, but I could barely talk. "So, was that your first adventure experience," the cameraman asked.

"Umm, I guess so."

"Yeah, you really freaked out! That's about the most scared I've ever seen someone!" Ugh, that really took the wind out of my chute. I knew I'd been a disaster but thought that was pretty common when jumping out of a damn plane!

Then it was Brook's turn to jump, and for the next thirty minutes I sat on a bench under a palm tree, watching the plane take off and then the tiny speck of Brook make his jump. I'm not going to lie and say that I was happy Brook encouraged me to face this fear. But I guess I was thankful in some ways. There aren't many people in our lives who can motivate us to do something so out of character. With Brook as my husband, I wanted him to push me to take risks and try new things. I flashed back to what the therapist said during the "Professional Advice" date: "Sometimes you just have to take a leap." I thought I should e-mail her to thank her for the pep talk and tell her that Brook and I were leaping twice—once out of a plane and once down the aisle.

DATE #38

Lessons in Divorce

JILL: That second leap would be at least as dangerous as the first. Back in D.C., at a noisy happy hour restaurant, we met my old boss Kurt, whose wife had just moved out of their house. They were getting a divorce.

I'd met Kurt at my first serious job after college, and we stayed in touch even after I moved on. I learned he'd met a woman around his age who worked as a lawyer and had a young daughter. They fell in love and Kurt went from being my older bachelor friend to a married husband and dad. It suited him. He seemed quite happy.

And then out of nowhere, I heard he was signing divorce papers. It was sad and surprising—How did a marriage go so bad so fast? During this intensely emotional time, Kurt graciously agreed to meet Brook and me for dinner to share what he'd learned. "And it's cheaper than therapy," he said with a laugh.

After half a glass of wine he started telling his marriage backstory, working over the clues he wished he'd noticed sooner. "We had all the conversations you're supposed to have," he said. "And she had all the right answers." He fingered his drink. They had met online and dated for less than a year before he proposed.

"The first couple of years were fun, it wasn't stressful, it wasn't a lot of work. In hindsight it was too easy. I talked to her first ex recently and it was the same thing for him. She started by being very supportive and available so it felt good, like you had a partner. And then there's just something where that flips with her. These were things that if we were dating for two or three years I would have noticed . . . But it was beyond my frame of reference that she wasn't being honest."

The mechanics of the marriage's demise weren't especially original: She liked to spend money, she lied about it, and Kurt's discovery of her dishonesty eroded their whole relationship. You could see on his face and in his slumped shoulders how sad Kurt was. He had found a partner, become a father to his stepdaughter, built a life with them, and now stood in the rubble of that collapsed family.

The lesson I took from Kurt's divorce was to push each other toward a painful level of honesty before signing on to forever. We all have a natural tendency to say what we think our mate wants to hear, so talking about these issues wasn't the same as truly facing them. I had always expected to be a supportive co-parent, but when we "Borrowed a Baby" I was actually pretty condescending to Brook. Our forty dates had been a gut check of whether our promises (to ourselves and our partner) matched our actions. I wasn't going to say it to Kurt, but I felt confident that Brook and I were not headed for the kind of surprises he was still trying to make sense of.

BROOK: Dinner came and then another round of drinks. I was curious when it started for Kurt, when he first had a sense that someone who seemed "supportive" and "fun" was actually "somewhere on the spectrum of 'not a good person.'"

"The flight back from the honeymoon was the first time I looked at her and was like, 'Who the hell are you?' We had gotten delayed and were finally in Atlanta for our connection and she was getting cranky in a way I hadn't seen before. It was after midnight and I asked her if we should look for a hotel and she just started barking at me, telling me to shut up. It was just out of proportion and I remember thinking, 'What the hell?' For some people once they get married they can be themselves, because you can't go anywhere. Buddies had told me how their wives had flipped out once they were married and I'm sitting there thinking, 'Oh my God, did I just marry that?'"

His wife was a needy, dishonest, bankrupt, antisocial, manipulative bad mother. That seemed to be the main point of his story. I felt bad for Kurt but also frustrated by his version of events. "She was never willing to take any responsibility," he said, taking none himself. I started to think his marriage might have been too bad to draw any larger lesson from, except not to get married until you're sure your partner isn't a psycho. But then we hit on one useful nugget.

Kurt explained that when he was growing up his father had a mercurial and abusive personality, and Kurt made sure to be nothing like his dad.

"Instead I ended up marrying someone like him," he said.

All of us mirror the relationships we've observed and been a part of, especially ones involving our parents. After Kurt's story, I gave a good think to the ways Jill's and my relationship is a version of our parents' marriages. When Jill filled a room with chatter and energy while I sat mainly silent, she was being my mom and I was being my dad. When Jill joked about how long it had been since I went grocery shopping, she was communicating in the way she'd seen growing up. Those weren't necessarily bad things, but they were worth remembering.

More than anything, Kurt reminded me how hard it is to know if you're marrying the right person until you've already married them. How was he supposed to know about the bankruptcy-level credit card debt his girlfriend kept racking up? Oh, that's right, he could have asked to see all her bank statements before they got married. In dozens of ways, Jill and I had done the hard, uncomfortable work of truly vetting our relationship, and I walked out of that dinner with an even greater appreciation for the value of what we'd put ourselves through.

DATE #39

They Made It Work

BROOK: There was another relationship Jill was interested in modeling ourselves after, a couple she had grown up across the street from and thought of as her adoptive grandparents. Dave and Sandi started dating their senior year of high school; their courtship was interrupted when Dave got drafted into the Korean War, but it was barely a speed bump.

> DAVE: I came home in March and we were married in June.
> SANDI: July.
> DAVE: Yeah, July third. Sometime in there.
> SANDI: It was Bastille Day.
> DAVE: Yeah, the fourteenth.
> SANDI: And we've been together ever since.

Now, fifty-eight years later, they invited us to chat at their kitchen table. Dave was increasingly worried that Sandi's memory was going—and it was—but they both easily recalled that first evening together.

> SANDI: I can remember what I wore. You took me to the nightclub, but we weren't old enough yet.
> DAVE: So I took you to Elmo's instead. She got all dressed up; she was beautiful but the first time she picked up ribs she dropped it down the front of her dress.
> SANDI: White dress. Right down the front.
> DAVE: It was an interesting night because I had broken my nose playing football and they couldn't repair it right away, so they had taken all the bone out and packed it with wax to keep the shape. So we were at the Palladium and it was very hot and I went into the men's room and washed my face and all of a sudden I pushed my nose and the wax went everywhere. So between her dropping the ribs on her dress and me with my nose . . .
> SANDI: But he did ask me out again. And I said, "Yes."

We talked for well over an hour about raising kids and being partners. Their most concrete advice was not especially romantic, which only made it ring more true.

"What made our marriage work is we both were fairly frugal before we married and we both brought some money to the wedding," Dave said. "And we always put away a little something every month. . . . We've been very fortunate because there's never been a period of financial problems, and I think that is the one thing that interferes with a lot of relationships."

Any couple that married in America in 1956 saw a lot of their friends divorce. I wondered, beyond money, what they'd seen go wrong with those relationships. "It was all different things," Dave said. "For every couple it's a bit different; you couldn't really point to one thing."

"Well, infidelity," Sandi said.

Dave and Sandi had some kind of amazing filter that seemed to only allow them to register the good parts of their life together. In the course of our conversation they mentioned how they had been forced to move to different cities seven times, how Dave's work schedule made him an absentee father, how their son had once gone fifteen years without speaking to him. But if any of these things were reasons to feel badly about their marriage, it didn't occur to them. They mentioned difficulties as if they were listing yesterday's specials at a favorite restaurant.

DAVE: It won't always be the way you want it.

SANDI: There will be concessions to make. That's part of life.

DAVE: There's going to be fights. Not really fights, disagreements. And that's rather normal. And they're easy to take care of. You have to work it out together and be honest.

SANDI: We just have been happy-go-lucky all the way through.

DAVE: Enjoy it and make it so you don't have to ever separate. Make it work.

JILL: As we sat there I found myself relating more to Dave's experience than Sandi's. Maybe it was a sign of the different gender expectations in their generation and ours.

"I was gone a lot traveling for work," Dave said. "I always felt bad about it because there were a lot of broken arms and a lot of piano recitals and a lot of football games I didn't make. I was gone."

My professional life could easily take me down that path as well. When I worked as a traveling consultant I flew to my client every Monday morning and returned home late Thursday. Even my new job pulled me out of town about one day a week. Very few mothers are in those types of jobs, and I often wondered if I could keep up that schedule as a wife and mom. Dave seemed to be saying he regretted missing so much.

"Sandi had to take on a lot of the household responsibility. And I always respected her for that." Women of my generation were trying to find a way to be both Dave and Sandi—consultant and mother, boss and wife, breadwinner and Band-Aid applier. By working so hard to do both jobs, maybe we ignored that we still had to choose which one we'd do best. David and Sandi reminded me that even two people could barely do it all.

Mostly though they talked about the good times, their camping trips and family adventures. "You've been lucky that your interests overlap a lot," Brook noted. "Or maybe you've overlapped more as you spent your life together?"

Dave nodded. "I think you're right, we probably overlapped a little when we married. I think now we're half of each other."

"It's a 'we' turned into one," Sandi added with a smile. It somehow wasn't an overly sentimental idea when they were the ones saying it.

"That's a good way to put it," Dave agreed. "The overlapping of the thoughts and the idea that you share the duties good and bad. We try to do that. Except for the cooking. She's not any good in the kitchen."

After fifty-eight years together they were still so clearly in love; they not only cared for one another, but they loved and respected each other. They were a billboard for the benefits and pleasures of building a life with someone. And yet even they wouldn't be together forever.

"This is my eighth decade," Dave said. "There's not a whole lot of years after eighty."

"There could be!" I pointed out.

"You don't know if that's good or bad," Dave said. Sandi now had some major health issues, and we were meeting them a few days before Dave's last hunting trip. "I just don't feel I can be away from her that long anymore; I'm responsible for her." Sandi protested, but it was clear: They had reached their last years together.

"We hope to make it to our sixtieth wedding anniversary; that's kind of a good goal," Dave said.

"That's easy, that's two years from now." Sandi laughed.

"Easy for you to say; I don't even buy green bananas anymore!" Dave joked. My heart broke. I imagined Brook and me in our eighties sitting at a table like this one. That was the best-case scenario, and even that felt fleeting.

DATE #40

Handcuffs

JILL: On the last Saturday morning of our forty dates, our life was still ahead of us. In two weeks we'd fly down to Costa Rica and make our public vows. All that stood between us and marriage was the most absurd date we'd dared put on the list: Brook and I were handcuffing ourselves together for twenty-four hours. We took the handcuffs out of their box and looked at the chain; it was maybe two inches long.

"Okay, I'm giving you my right hand," Brook said. It was a chivalrous sacrifice to lock up his dominant arm. I guess we would have been more compatible if one of us were left-handed.

We noted the time—11:41 A.M.—and locked ourselves in. "Where should we go?" he asked. We walked over to the couch and sat there together reading for a while. I was a bit antsy to do something but didn't want to make Brook get up for no real reason, so we sat there silently side by side, not able to move apart and not really needing to.

"Maybe we should make some lunch," I said. "It's going to take a while." Yes, we had improved as a couple in the kitchen, but now we'd be working with just two free arms. Brook started chopping with his shackled right hand, while I tried using my left to grab something out of a drawer. "Hold off on the chopping for a minute." Making lunch was dangerous but actually digesting it was truly terrifying, for biological reasons you may have already considered.

I remember my high school volleyball coach telling our team one day that she was going to miss a lot of our practices. "My husband fell off a ladder yesterday and broke both his arms," she said. "He has double casts and won't be able to take care of himself for a few weeks."

"How does he go to the bathroom?" we wanted to know.

"Well, um, I'm going to have to help him wipe and stuff." We were *horrified*.

When Brook closed the handcuff around my left wrist I flashed back to that feeling. We were about to experience the truth that sometimes in married life shit happens. I really really really *really* hoped I wouldn't have to go to the bathroom in front of Brook, but I had come up with a backup plan.

"I have an idea," I told him. "If one of us has to use the bathroom"—I emphasized the word *bathroom* to make clear I didn't mean peeing—"then the other can wear a blindfold and headphones." He laughed and said sure.

About an hour after we ate, Brook turned to me as if he were ten months pregnant and announced, "I think it's time." I would never be emotionally ready for this, but I was physically prepared with a necktie and headphones. We shuffled into the bathroom and I did my best to busy my mind with pretty much anything else. It was over before I knew it.

That night we headed to bed and awkwardly lay down on our backs. An attempt to spoon led to tangled limbs, so there could be no tossing and turning. That's not to say I fell asleep right away. My mind was racing. The Marriage Test had been the single biggest personal project I'd ever done. For months this was how I spent my free time, what I thought about when I was alone, and what I talked about at parties. I had cried, cheered, screamed, swooned. The stakes had been so high.

Through it all Brook was there as my partner and supporter, the only person I knew who would want to start a project like this, and the only man I had ever met whom I would want to finish it with. We had come out the other side as a different couple than the Jill and Brook who walked separately through the rain to that first date at the Hyatt. Now we lay there in handcuffs, comfortably together. We were the Jill and Brook who had proved they trusted each other and could work together to achieve their goals, a couple who had found an honest understanding of their relationship's problems and practiced how to overcome them.

I wanted to celebrate with a huge party or a giant Publishers Clearing House fake check to prove what a monumental thing this was. But instead, we would celebrate with the kind of small moment the rest of our lives would be built on: walking across V Street to discover Tacos El Chilango and playing softball after work on the grass below the Washington Monument. I finally fell asleep picturing the beach, me in a white dress, the future both unknown and secure.

BROOK: I was surprised how well we slept. I woke first and needed to pee but lay there for a while waiting for her to stir. We had another three hours joined at the wrist. "You're up," she said finally. We rolled awkwardly toward each other for a kiss. We were both wearing sweatshirts because once you're handcuffed to someone you can't change clothes.

When we finally rose from bed, Jill turned respectfully as I peed and I sat on the bathroom windowsill when it was her turn. Roosevelt was right, your fear of pretty much anything is worse than what you feel when you do it.

It seemed like cheating to stay in our apartment for twenty-four hours, so we decided to go grocery shopping. We couldn't put coats on over the handcuffs, so we wore them as shawls and made the walk up Fourteenth Street to the market. It was hard to say how many people noticed that we were handcuffed, but it wasn't none of them.

There were stares and laughs as we walked across P Street. I felt kind of separated from the rest of the city, much too embarrassed to talk to anyone except the checkout lady. It felt like a bubble separated the two of us from everyone else, that it was us against the world.

I didn't believe in soul mates, at least not if that meant there was only one person you were destined to be with. Finding that one person would be impossible! No, I always believed our lives could take a million paths, turned by small moments and big choices. It was easy to imagine living somewhere else, having a different job, even loving another person.

But when you believed your life could go so many different ways, and you were approaching the most important milestone of the whole damn trip, you couldn't help but turn back and take a long look at the twisted road that brought you there.

My mental list of turns on the path to Jill usually started with my friend Katie telling me about the party in Boston where her friends were meeting up. I was invited because I was living with my parents in Rhode Island at the time, because I had just gotten back from that big trip around the world. I remembered running to catch the last train to Boston at the station in Bridgewater, Massachusetts. And then later that night, at a house in the suburbs, the girl with blue eyes and brown curls got in the first cab to the bar, and I sat on that porch in Quincy for ninety minutes waiting for a second cab to come. How different my life might be if Jill and I had gotten in the same car and gotten to know each other in some different way.

I thought about the night I asked Jill to be my girlfriend, and the night I broke up with her. I thought about the afternoons in therapy and the one session I walked out of terribly distraught. I called her number by memory; she picked up and listened. She even came to my New Year's party when she shouldn't have, and walked me back down off the roof after midnight. Actually, I guess it started on a New Year's Eve way before that. Half a dozen of us walking up Second Avenue on the last night of 2003. "Let's go in here," I said as we passed Fáilte. It was an Irish pub I'd never been in, and when the bartender handed me a pint, a stranger knocked it over. That was how I met Katie.

In that way, you could see how the idea of soul mates made sense. So many things had to go right for us to end up together! But we weren't soul mates based on some cosmic plan but rather from the sediment of all our lives' choices, our worst moments and best efforts, the promises we kept and the forgiveness we gave. Soul mates weren't found, they were made. And knowing that was also a burden. It meant we weren't destined for happiness or compatibility on any page beyond this one. We unlocked the handcuffs and felt what held us together.

Epilogue

The guests, sweating in slacks and long sleeves, walked down the palm-lined path to the beach. We had arranged twenty chairs near the shore and by the power vested in her by the Internet, Katie would marry us eight years after introducing us.

We had already survived our first wedding reception in Rhode Island, held two months before in September for the sake of the weather. A hundred East Coast friends gathered by the water on a sunny Saturday; at dusk we sent wish lanterns over the Jamestown Bridge. It was lovely. And by the time we left for Costa Rica, most of the details for the upcoming West Coast party had been finalized—the paella guy and the photographer were already booked.

But our week in Costa Rica was built on volunteer labor. Everyone took a turn cooking a meal; a group of us went fishing for the wedding dinner. In between, Steve and Brook played catch on the beach, while Jason and Paige nearly learned how to surf.

Quite suddenly, it was time for us to walk down to the shore. First

Brook with his mom, then Jill with her dad. Around the end of the palm path, she turned onto the beach in a thin-strapped cream dress that left long crescent curves in the sand. The chain of her GVA necklace tangled with the GSB pendant she'd just unwrapped. As she came into view, Brook broke into tears that continued through Katie's welcome and the reading of the couple's first e-mails to each other and Brook's dad singing "Home" by Edward Sharpe. Then finally the vows, which the bride had insisted should include the phrase "till death do us part." Brook went first:

Jill, you are the best thing that's ever happened to me.
I've never met anyone who is so adventurous, funny,
    smart, patient, beautiful, and caring.
You inspire me to be a better version of myself.
You show faith in me even when I lack faith in myself.
You always know where my keys are.
I am certain you will be an amazing mother and loving
    partner.
I promise to be your faithful husband and build a family
    with you,
I promise to love and support you even when things are
    bad, but to work to make them mainly good.
I promise to help you live the life you've dreamed of,
    and the life that together we'll discover we want.
I promise to be your best friend till death do us part.

❧

BSB—a day with you is never dull.
You are so loving, so supportive, and so damn fun
    that my mind, body, and spirit are constantly fulfilled.

With you I really have met my match.
I've found a partner whose patience, thoughtfulness,
        and creativity complement who I am.
Together we're an awesome team.
I can't imagine a better father for my children and
        man by my side till death do us part.
As your wife: I promise to stay interesting, intellectually,
        physically, and socially,
I promise to love your family as I love my own,
I promise to be honest and faithful to our marriage,
And I promise to continue to say, "Yes, and . . ." keeping
        our life full of spontaneity and just shy of crazy.
I love you, Brook.

Back home in D.C. we still weren't married. The Costa Rican ceremony wasn't recognized in the United States, so we arrived at Family Court Marriage Bureau Room 4485 at 3:30 P.M. on the Monday
after we got home. If you added this appointment to the ceremony
on the beach and the two receptions, we had stumbled into a fourth
wedding. A Portuguese interpreter who was on his break walked
in—he would be the officiant. "Wilt thou have this person to be thy
wedded spouse?"

"I will."

"I will."

It was 4:15 P.M. on a November afternoon and we were finally
married. "You hungry?" the bride asked. We went up to the Fainting
Goat, a restaurant on U Street we'd never tried, and ordered a couple
of cocktails. At the next table a guy was sitting alone with an
untouched cheese plate. It looked good so we ordered one of those too.

"Hi, you must be Mark," a woman said as she took the seat across from the cheese plate guy. She had been held up at work, but it was okay, he hadn't been waiting long.

We tried not to eavesdrop, but they were kind of cute. A few minutes before they had never set eyes on one another, and in a few months they might be closer to each other than they were to their immediate families. The Fainting Goat started to feel like a high school we had just graduated from, and here were the freshmen, clueless and anxious, with so much big stuff still to experience.

We'd like to say we called the waiter over and picked up their check and left a note wishing them well, but Mr. and Mrs. Silva-Braga just walked out onto U Street together.

YOUR TURN

You know you want to try it. We designed the Marriage Test to be easily accessible to any couple, so most of the dates cost next to nothing and can be done in or near your home. We think anyone can benefit from the forty dates, but they're especially geared toward couples auditioning each other for the Big Job and for engaged partners looking to start their marriage on a strong note (or just looking for an excuse to avoid wedding planning).

If your Marriage Test gets uncomfortable, good! That's the point. Don't skip dates just because they sound scary. If you don't have time for all forty, try taking turns nominating five or ten dates each. Try a date from each category—a Daters' Decathlon. Or focus on one category exclusively. Or invent your own. Remember, the point is to really live whatever you're trying to learn about.

Having spent a year road-testing all these dates, we have some tips to make them go smoothly . . . but don't worry, they won't go that smoothly:

Trust

#1—SPEED DATING

Plan to spend at least $35 and two hours testing your devotion to one another. A quick Internet search should get you there. Arrive separately with some clearly defined ground rules, which should probably include no follow-up messages once you leave the den of temptation. Plan a rendezvous and debrief afterward to talk over whatever trouble you've gotten yourselves into.

#2—PHONE SWAP

Trade phones for forty-eight hours. You might want to set some ground rules that could range from only letting each other look at stuff from when you've been dating to only allowing access to certain things (i.e., e-mails but not texts; Twitter but not Facebook). We impersonated each other in our replies to inbound messages, which led to some funny moments, but proceed with caution.

#3—MEET THE EXES

Go out with each other's exes, ideally as a group of four (we had to do it separately). You really need to emphasize to your ex how cool they are for doing this. Schedule it somewhere convenient for them. Make sure everyone is totally over each other. Lunch was the right length and tone for our dates. Make sure to pick up the tab.

Money

#4—TRADING CREDIT CARDS

You're swapping credit cards for a month so you can only buy things with the other's money. Also exchange about $100 cash to use for things you can't charge, then give back what's left at the end of the month. Don't peek at your bank balance; it's more fun (and a more useful exercise) to spend their money without knowing how they're spending yours. We didn't have any trouble using each other's cards except when purchasing a plane ticket. Our solution: Keep track of any charge that absolutely must be put on your personal card. Then get reimbursed at the end of the month.

#5—BUDGET CRUNCH

For a month you can only spend half of what you normally do. Adding up your "regular" expenses can be enlightening and difficult; it took us about an hour to calculate a year's total and divide by twelve to get a fair average. We didn't include rent, or Jill's school loans, because it's not practical to reduce them on short notice for a month. You might feel the same about car payments or health insurance. We equally divided our "budget," but you could decide to give one person more to spend. Check in every week or so to see what's left and plan accordingly.

#6—FULL DICLOURE

You're revealing all your bank balances to each other—credit cards, loans, savings, etc. Give yourself an hour to gather your financial statements on paper or online before you start sharing; it takes some time to get them all in one place. We made a spreadsheet in Excel to tally our totals and possibly update in the future. We spent $15 to access our scores at myFICO.com, but many credit cards now offer it free of charge. You can set a prize for the higher score like a massage or dinner, or you can go big like we did and put final wedding budget decisions in the winner's hands.

Kids

#7—BORROWING A BABY

You're taking care of a real, live child for twenty-four hours. We happened to have access to a nine-month-old, but almost any kid will do! An offer of twenty-four hours of free babysitting turns out to be pretty attractive, so it may be easier to borrow a baby than you think. Venture outside during your parenting session to see just how hard it really is. If you've always pictured carrying your spawn to brunch, give it a try.

#8—SOUNDS LIKE A NEWBORN

You're signing up for a week of sleeplessness, setting an alarm to wake you up every three hours during the night. Before going back to bed, you'll have to do a chore you pull out of a hat. *Bounce your baby for ten minutes. Go to a store and buy milk. Do a load of laundry. Walk around the block with your baby. Cook a meal. Organize your cabinets.* You'll need a "baby"—we chose a watermelon. Add your own tasks to the ones we mentioned; they're allowed to be useful, like cleaning your bathroom. Any chore that goes faster if you both help is especially . . . interesting. And no naps!

#9—TIMELINE

Separately create timelines for your future—when you'd want to have kids, move cities, buy a home, get married, and so on. Make sure to include anything else that will shape and define your life in the future. Jill added in a student loan payoff estimate, since that plays a big part in our budget over the next few years. Then compare and discuss where you're in sync and where you aren't.

#10—LOSING MY RELIGION

You're deciding what religion, if any, you'll raise your children in. Start by experiencing your options. If you're religious, bring your partner to an upcoming service. If you grew up religious but are nonpracticing today, attend a service to introduce them to what you experienced as a kid. Get into the details. "Yeah, I want to raise my kids Catholic" is not specific enough. Do you want to go to church every week? Would you want your partner to join? Will your kids receive the sacraments?

Sex

#11—SEX NOTES

After a week of your best efforts, exchange feedback on what is and isn't working in the bedroom. You could hold your own private Reddit-style "Ask Me Anything," or create sexual "Wish Lists" to swap and discuss. Remember, compliment sandwiches can help soften the blow of tougher feedback!

#12—NOT THAT AGAIN

Your assignment is to have sex every day for a week without repeating the same act twice. This can be as elaborate or simple as you want. Sex outside? That counts. Adventures with elbows? Now's the time. We didn't plan what we would do in advance, but you might want to. Or just put some ideas in a hat and pull one (or more!) each night. If you have trouble coming up with ideas, buy an adventurous sex book, watch some porn, or read erotica. Better yet, do all of that.

#13—CAN'T TOUCH THIS

Don't touch each other, at all, for a week. If you share a bed and it's not that big, you may need to erect some kind of barrier. We brushed each other a few times in our sleep, but it didn't seem to undo the enlightening effects of not touching while we were awake.

#14—SEX SEEN

For two weeks you're re-creating whatever sex scenes you watch together, so HBO, R-rated movies, foreign films . . . they're all great sources of cinema for this date. Get creative with how you reenact each scene, just make sure you do it soon after you see it—we tried to remake the film within a day. Some would argue part of the fun is gaming the system and picking things you already know you want to reenact. And there's no reason you have to stop after two weeks.

In-Laws, Etc.

#15—IN-LAW HANDBOOK

You're looking to spend time with someone who has married into your partner's family, or at least come close. If at all possible do this date in person and buy a round of drinks. Definitely do not invite your partners along. If you don't have siblings or in-laws available, start looking for aunts/uncles/cousins until you find someone who has dared to date into the family. You don't need to tell your partner what was shared.

#16—IN-LAW PEN PALS

Every day for two weeks you need to contact someone in your partner's family; ideally as many different people as possible. E-mails, phone calls, texts all count. Don't tell your families about the date, just let them enjoy hearing from you.

#17—STAND-INS

Nominate two close friends to play you and your partner and set aside about an hour for their performance. They don't need to know each other. You want to see how your friends perceive your relationship, so have them act out a range of different situations (financial, family, work, etc.) as suggested by you or your assembled friends. Try to find a somewhat private space for the date. A crowded bar or restaurant probably wouldn't be the best setting.

#18—SURVEY SAYS

You're anonymously surveying friends and family about their feelings toward your relationship. We set up our survey for free at Survey Monkey.com. Use the feedback to help shape other dates you should do or things you should discuss before finishing your Marriage Test. Feel free to steal some of the questions we used:

- What do you think are the best things about Jill and Brook as a couple?
- What do you think are the biggest weaknesses of Jill and Brook as a couple?
- How can Jill be a better partner to Brook?
- How can Brook be a better partner to Jill?
- How compatible are Jill and Brook? A great match, Pretty good together, Good enough I guess, They're not right for each other.
- If you had to predict what will cause the most tension in their relationship, it would be: Finances, Raising children, Work, Sexual compatibility, In-laws, Religion, Housekeeping, Other.
- In public or group settings, Jill and Brook: Show too much affection, Show too little affection, Bicker too much, Act boring, Get too loud/outspoken, Act about right.
- Should Jill and Brook get married?
- What other feedback or advice can you offer?

#19—IN-LAW BUCKET LIST

Asking your potential in-laws their hopes for their child can be pretty intense. Try to talk with them in person and spend at least thirty minutes chatting. You can offer your own list of dreams for your partner, but try to have them do most of the talking. This is also a good chance to talk about any health concerns you or they might have, like depression or undiagnosed issues.

Communication

#20—TEST YOUR LOVE

The Internet abounds with all manner of relationship quizzes. We chose two classics: The 5 Love Languages and Myers-Briggs, both of which you can take online. These are popular for a reason. Even the random broken relationship compatibility quiz we found prompted an interesting discussion, so you probably can't go wrong by just trying out a few different ones.

#21—SILENT NIGHT

Pretty simple. Don't talk for an evening, or a full day if you're truly daring. We communicated via gestures and grunts, but banned handwritten notes (you may want to allow them). Staying in that night meant there were no opportunities to talk to others. We didn't turn on music or TV sound, so it really was a completely silent night.

#22—IT'S A CHORE

If you live together, walk through your home room by room, separately writing down what you think needs to be cleaned or tidied. If you live separately you can still do this at each of your homes and focus on how the other helps with or contributes to the mess. Aim to identify mismatches in what each of you considers clean and dirty. Questions like "Is it time to take out the garbage yet?" or "Does this need to be cleaned now?" will help prompt that conversation. You'll be more successful than we were if you're able to turn this conversation into a game plan for future cleanliness.

#23—PLAY IT BACK

Record a fight or emotional conversation—you can wait for one to emerge organically or just record "It's a Chore" or another date you expect to be contentious. We used a video camera, but a cell phone voice memo will work fine too. Once the dust settles, give a listen, possibly separately at first, but also ultimately together. You can stop to point out things or ask questions if you like, but don't interrupt too much. Once you've both had a chance to listen and reflect, try to discuss ways to argue more constructively.

#24—PROFESSIONAL ADVICE

Go to at least one session of couples counseling. Many employer health insurance plans have an employee assistance program (EAP) or mental health benefit that will get you a few free therapy sessions per year. If you don't have insurance, you could consider low-cost mental health clinics or premarriage counseling through your faith or community organization.

Quality Time

#25—BLACKOUT BY DESIGN

You can't use any electronics outside of work hours for a week—we set aside 6 P.M. to 7 A.M. as our blackout zone. Tell your families and relevant coworkers so they understand when you're unresponsive. Since the goal is to really connect, make sure most of your time is spent with just the two of you. Oh, and the idea is to remove digital distractions, so feel free to use your lights and electric stove.

#26—TIME WELL SPENT

For a week, each of you should track how you spend time together—not just what you do but whether you feel it was rewarding. Then go back and look for trends in what you've done and how you've felt. Debrief afterward to identify what enhances and undermines your relationship, then work to create more of what you both value.

#27—YOU'RE IN CHARGE

You're taking turns telling each other how to spend your time. Set aside at least two days for this date so you each have an opportunity to be the boss—better yet, set aside a whole week and take turns. This is your chance to force your partner to do all the things you always hoped they would. If you're just doing one day each, you might want to map out your plans ahead of time to avoid revenge from whoever bosses second. Of course, you can only plan their free time; work hours are off limits unless you plan to replace their income should they get fired.

#28—YOUR IDEAL DAY

Just like it sounds. Take turns planning a day your partner will love. It doesn't have to be elaborate or expensive. Show your love by demonstrating that you've been listening and that you understand their tastes and preferences.

Partnership

#29—ROAD TRIP PACKING LIST

You're packing each other's bags without help. Plan to be gone at least a weekend so you each have to account for a few scenarios. And don't give each other hints! Raise the stakes by agreeing not to purchase or share anything that wasn't packed. Your boyfriend forgot to pack toothpaste, no toothpaste for you!

#30—QUIZ TIME

You're each creating a twenty-question quiz on a topic of importance to you while studying for your partner's test. Jill chose her home state; Brook picked his favorite sports team. Everything you include needs to be facts you already know; no researching to build your quiz. Agree on a prize for the winner and break out the #2 pencils. Our actual quiz only took about fifteen minutes.

#31—TEACH ME WHAT YOU DO

Executing this date will vary widely depending on what jobs you each have. Plan to spend about thirty minutes to an hour showing your partner what an average day looks like, teaching them relevant jargon, or showing them how to complete a task that's central to your job. They should come away with a great answer to "So what does your partner do for work?"

#32—PERSONALITY SWAP

Assume each other's identities for an afternoon or evening—the good and the bad. Bonus points if you dress like them or adopt their mannerisms. FYI, this date is very likely to cause hurt feelings, so consider this your warning!

Marriage Prep

#33—HOW WILL WE SAY "I DO"?

Plan to spend roughly one hour discussing each of your general wedding visions. This is probably not the time to pick out your wedding colors or first dance song (though if you already have strong preferences, let your partner know). Mainly, this is your chance to see if you're on the same page about the basics—location(s), invitees (twenty, one hundred, or five hundred?), and budget (four, five, or six figures?). Trust us, you'll have plenty of time to discuss details if you do end up heading down the aisle.

#34—TAKE MY NAME

You're trading last names to help decide what you'll call yourselves if you get married. Start by setting up new e-mail accounts, updating social media, and calling each other by your "swapped" names.

Remember to sign your new signature after every purchase. We switched names for two weeks, but you could probably get value in only seven days.

#35—DOWNER DOCS

You're discussing the lousy, legal realities of joining lives—a pre-nup, living will, and financial family support. Plan to spend at least thirty minutes on each. These are tough and emotional chats, so be prepared for that. And feel free to add other topics. This is your chance to talk about the things you'd rather avoid. Better bring them up now!

#36—HOUSE HUNTING

You're looking for a house you'd want to buy together. Spend about thirty minutes talking specifics—size, location, price tag, features—to narrow down the type of house you both want. Your local paper, Zillow.com, and Craigslist.com will all have open house listings to choose from. And feel free to do this date even if you're not located in the area where you expect to buy. Just focus on discussing elements of what you're looking for in a home.

The Long Haul

#37—FACING OUR FEARS

Nominate fears for each other to overcome—or better yet, find something you're both scared of and face it together! This could get pricey (it was our most expensive date by far), but it doesn't have to.

#38—LESSONS IN DIVORCE

Take a divorced friend out for dinner and/or drinks. Be a good listener—both to support them and to find themes in their marriage that sound familiar in your relationship. Ask what they would do differently if they had to do it all over again.

#39—THEY MADE IT WORK

Find a couple who has managed to stay (happily) married for a long time. We chose former neighbors who were probably able to speak so freely because we didn't have many mutual acquaintances. Our chat took about an hour, so you can easily do it over lunch or cocktails one day.

#40—HANDCUFFS

You're handcuffing yourselves together for twenty-four hours! Take a trip to your local adult entertainment store and pick up a set of handcuffs ($20). Or be boring and buy them from Amazon. Pick out clothes you don't mind keeping on for a full day—including a bra—since there's no way to take anything off your chest once you're locked in. Perhaps get a blindfold and headphones ready for any bathroom visits that you'd rather not fully experience. It's up to you if you can handle the inevitable stares that *will* happen if you venture out in public.

ACKNOWLEDGMENTS

We'd like to start by thanking the program that auto-wrote this book for us. Because of you, we didn't have to spend our first months as newlyweds battling over how to describe our breakup in these pages. Brook never had to tell Jill, "That joke isn't funny," and Jill never had to tell Brook, "That story isn't interesting." Without you, AutoWriter2000, it's unlikely our marriage would have survived the flight home from Costa Rica.

Thanks to the power of auto-book writing, we have no need to thank Rafe Sagalyn, Leah Culler, Amanda Mansour, Tristan Bannon, Heather Scott, Madeline Perez, Drew Mackie, Jennifer Frosch, Jessica Jarahian, Dori Logiodice, Sophia Lambertsen, Brent Shannon, or Allison Elliott-Shannon for offering feedback on early drafts.

Our editor, Denise Silvestro, and agent, Kari Stuart, certainly would have had their work cut out for them had we actually struggled to shape a story and choose a direction for the project.

But for all of its considerable narrative gifts, the AW2000 could not have crafted such a delicate and humanlike story if not for our family and friends. For over a year they helped us create and refine date ideas, then execute and document them—from Sheila and Xandy Bustamante suggesting we pack each other's bags to Matt McFarland following us down Fourteenth Street with a video camera as we awkwardly carried his coffee in our handcuffed hands.

We didn't want to fill the book with statistics or expert advice; we relied on the honesty of ordinary people to animate the challenge of pairing off. Relationships are hard to talk about, so our biggest thanks should go to the couples and singles who shared their stories with us.

Finally, it's hard to imagine we could have passed our Marriage Test if our parents hadn't passed it first. Jan and Tom Andres and John Braga and Nancy Silva have inspired and supported us since that first moment we recognized two people could be partners, but not without work.

ABOUT THE AUTHORS

Jill Andres is a business consultant who helps companies invent new products, from cereal and stereos to tractors and windowpanes. In her free time, she loves discovering tasty restaurant deals, reading in parks, and sneaking episodes of *The Real Housewives*.

Brook Silva-Braga is a journalist and filmmaker whose work has aired on HBO, CBS, MTV, and National Geographic. Born and raised in Rhode Island, he's traveled to more than fifty countries on six continents while rarely missing a New England Patriots game. He's never watched *The Real Housewives*.